Let's Buy Goats

Succeed in Business by avoiding these 60 pitfalls!

By Geoff Anderson

This book is a work of the author's experience and opinion.

This e-book is licensed for your personal enjoyment only. This e-book may not be re-sold or given away to other people. Copyright © 2021 Geoff Anderson.

All rights reserved, including the right to reproduce this book, or portions thereof, in any form. No part of this text may be reproduced, transmitted, downloaded, decompiled or stored in or introduced into any information storage and retrieval system, in any form or by any means, whether electronic or mechanical without the express written permission of the author.

The publisher does not have any control over and does not assume any responsibility for author or third-party websites or their content.

This book does not constitute legal, financial or insurance consultancy advice and must not be relied on as definitive in these areas. The book does recommend seeking professional advice for all these areas.

Contact the author at geoff@passioinateprofit.co.uk

ISBN: 9798544037231

Let's Buy Goats! 6

My Entrepreneurial Journey 10

Structure 15

Section One - The Heart of your Business 16

'The root of business failure rarely lies with actions taken but rather in your omissions'. 17

Pitfall 1 - The Absence of Need 18

Pitfall 2 - An idea out of Time 20

Pitfall 3 - An Idea that misses the Business Cycle 21

Pitfall 4 - Failure to Establish Brand 22

Pitfall 5 A Lack of Excitement 25

Section Two Getting Started 27

Pitfall 6 - Choosing the wrong Business 28

Pitfall 7 - An inappropriate Legal Structure 38

Pitfall 8 - A Bad Business Name 40

Pitfall 9 - Maintaining an Employee Mentality 44

Pitfall 10 The Wrong Business Partners 45

Pitfall 11 A Reluctance to Learn 47

Pitfall 12 The Wrong Motivation 51

Section Three Business Planning 54

Pitfall 13 A Lack of Paper Planning 59

Pitfall 14 A Failure to Grasp the Big Picture 81

Pitfall 15 A Failure to Introduce Scalability 84

Pitfall 16 Poor Strategy 86

Pitfall 17 Inability to Create a Money Machine 89

Pitfall 18 A Lack of Ambition 91

Pitfall 19 Taking the Wrong Advice 93

Pitfall 20 Failure to Manage the Downside 95

Pitfall 21 The Paralysis of Analysis 97

Pitfall 22 A Hobby not a Business 99

Pitfall 23 A Failure to Fully Utilize Assets 101

Pitfall 24 A Reluctance to be Flexible 104

Pitfall 25 A Failure to Align with your Suppliers 106

Section Four Marketing and Sales 108

Pitfall 26 Limited Product Lines 114

Pitfall 27 A Failure to Develop Your Product 117

Pitfall 28 A Failure to Understand your Market 119

Pitfall 29 Working with Bad Customers 123

Pitfall 30 A Reluctance to Sell 125

Pitfall 31 An Over Reliance on the Web 129

Pitfall 32 A Failure to Track Competition 131

Section Five Operations and Administration 132

Pitfall 33 A Failure to Give Time to your Objectives 136

Pitfall 34 A Failure of Governance 138

Pitfall 35 A Failure to take The Right Action 139

Pitfall 36 Over Working / Over delivering 143

Pitfall 37 A Failure to Manage Reputation 144

Pitfall 38 The Monster Within 146

Pitfall 39 Poor Time Management 147

Pitfall 40 Butterflying 149

Pitfall 41 Reinventing the Wheel 150

Pitfall 42 A Reluctance to Decline Work 152

Pitfall 43 Poor Scheduling of Work 153

Pitfall 44 A Failure to Comprehensively Cost 154

Pitfall 45 A Failure to Charge Enough 159

Pitfall 46 Poor Commercial Process 161

Pitfall 47 Failure to Use Professional Advice 165

Pitfall 48 Beware the Cerberus 167

Pitfall 49 Ignoring Legalities 170

Pitfall 50 A Failure to Manage Risk 171

Pitfall 51 A Failure to Insure 173

Pitfall 52 A Failure to Manage Profits 177

Pitfall 53 A Failure to Recruit Well 179
Section 6. Finance 181
Pitfall 54 Parsimony 185
Pitfall 55 Over Stocking 187
Pitfall 56 Failure to Manage Costs 190
Pitfall 57 Bad Cash Flow 192
Pitfall 58 Bad Debt Control 196
Pitfall 59 A Lack of Capital 199
Pitfall 60 Lack of Sustainability 201
My Offer to You 201

Let's Buy Goats!

I worked for Shell in Sarawak in the 90s. I was employed in the Operations Contracts Department tendering and awarding drilling and petrophysics contracts, my area of expertise, at that time.

In the next office, worked my close friend Neil. Neil was younger and new to the field. Neil covered the general contracts which included base maintenance. The grass cutting contracts were his least favorite task. Most of our contractors were international oil service companies, others were local Chinese owned contractors' but the grass cutting contracts were performed by local tribesmen. Their bids were poorly specified, and Neil's primary task was to assess whether the bidder could complete the work at the prices and using the methods proposed.

There would be about 20 bidders. Neil would start by eliminating the complete no-hopers and then start discussions with the lowest bidder. The process required two interpreters, one to translate from the tribal dialect to Bahasa Malay, the second from Bahasa to English.

I particularly remember one occasion.

The bidders all had little prospect of doing the work. The owners heard that money was to be made from Shell. For the jungle tribes, international oil companies were a complete mystery and their commercial processes.

The rest of us laughed unsympathetically at poor Neil. A kind, thoughtful guy, he did his best to coach the bidders through the process. I remember once, the first 6 tenderers, plus several iterations of the lowest bidder, were eliminated for various reasons. Some proposals the bidder's wife and daughters with hand sickles He was down to the last few the bidders. With no resolution they were each eliminated. His internal customer the production manager attended this final hopeless discussion and threw his hands up in exasperation saying:

'Let's buy goats!'

Not the worst idea. The locals bought goats, tied them up, and they would graze inside a circle the radius of the rope.

Shell did not adopt this route. The goat strategy would have been time consuming, staking and moving the goats and ensuring their health. We would be undertaking the work ourselves. It would cost more money, take more staff time and produced an inferior result

We coached one of the Chinese contractors to do the work by employing the tribal work force. This provided us with a reasonable managed solution.

It is the same challenge, I notice, with some tradesmen around my home. I hasten to add that I do not consider any of them to be goats!

These tradesmen are in every way skilled and expert in the work they do. Why should good commercial practice be any more familiar to them as they start out in business than for our Malaysian workforce.

As a contract professional through my career, I explained commercial process to engineers, drillers and senior management. Their knowledge of commercial practice was scant. My knowledge of their specialities equally patchy. Work around my home presents a similar situation.

I complete some work myself never in the time or to the quality of a professional, I get distracted by other priority things to do. I could employ the local 'jobber' but they might not possess the skills, have the insurance cover or knowledge to complete the work.

I could just employ these 'goats' but too many bodged jobs by goats appear on the TV, showcasing desperate customers; stranded, upset and out-of-pocket, roofs open to the weather, loft conversions incomplete, abandoned extensions, leaking plumbing, hanging cables, unfinished ceilings and walls, presenting a sorry scene.

The unfortunate residents plead with experts to rescue them.

You can easily see that whilst offering a tempting and innovative solution buying goats seldom works. You, the tradesperson being the goat is also an unsuccessful contracting approach. You take pride in the work that you do. Take the same pride and care in your commercial processes. I earnestly hope this book helps you to do this.

I write this book to address the issue that many new businesses fail because their owners understand and are expert at their trade but show a poor understanding of the associated commercial processes. Why would they?

I cannot wire my house. My joinery is fair at best but compared to a professional is shoddy. A time served painter, if such a thing still exists, finishes the work of all other trades to a standard and quality that I could never achieve.

There are currently over 5 million SME's - Small to Medium Enterprises in the UK. They account for 99% of UK businesses. Recent years have seen a rapid rise in entrepreneurship. The number of businesses increasing by some 300,000 a year, with many seeking the benefits that self-employment offers. Many heavily hit by the coronavirus lock down are struggling. Some have failed.

Entrepreneurship can be a lonely road which offers apparent control of one's own destiny, the possibility of future wealth and an end to the 9 to 5 and dancing to someone else's tune. This undoubtedly has attractions, but it is a road strewn with challenges. Over 250,000 of these businesses fail each year.

This is 9% of all businesses at present. A much larger percentage fail to get beyond 5-years. Many survive year one but fail as time passes and money, ideas and enthusiasm run out. The pandemic has made matters worse and will continue its impact for years to come

Business failure can be a personal tragedy and can result in far-reaching consequences for family, customers, suppliers and employees.

Those who survive will develop business skills which endure. Many aspiring entrepreneurs fail to achieve the income and security and rewards that entrepreneurship seemed to promise in those exciting early days.

Achieving these benefits is neither rare nor particularly difficult. In too many cases the challenges could be avoided with more knowledge, advice and guidance. Entrepreneurs rarely fail for their lack of effort.

Watching business TV programmes such as Dragons Den and the Apprentice, getting it right seems obvious to those experienced hands. Getting it wrong, seems to be the fate of the journeymen and women until they are touched by the successful with their knowledge, networks and cash.

This book is designed to give you advice on the pitfalls and the means to avoid them. I am committed to your success. For me there is nothing more enjoyable than to see a young entrepreneur succeed or an old one for that matter.

I enjoy many of the nice things in life, homes, travel, security. I coached and mentored many others in whose success I take greater pleasure. I ran multi-million-pound businesses grown from nothing. I serviced a global client base which I coached, trained and advised. For many years I loved every minute of my working life. There were setbacks, problems, disputes and disappointments. Without setbacks the best times would be less sweet however the majority of enjoyable times far outweighed the bad times. Without that favorable balance I would have stopped or worse had a breakdown.

Business today has become much more complex. Learning from mistakes is the road to failure as economics become less favourable and there is less room to ride the storm to eventual success.

I wrote this book in a way to help avoid sufficient of the potholes to tip the balance in your favors.

I wish you well in your endeavors. Let me know about your success.

My Entrepreneurial Journey

It was always likely that I would enter the world of business. My father ran the family business, a paint, wallpaper and glass wholesaler. He employed painters, glaziers and more trades. He held a royal warrant for work done on Balmoral Castle. Every Saturday and Sunday morning, I accompanied him to his business, and I sat with a typewriter writing sports reports for my newspaper which I sold at school.

I remember my father working long hours, taking calls at weekends and in the evening. I saw that the rewards were substantial but that these went with hard work, long hours and a commitment to his customers many of whom became close friends.

My earliest memory of a business venture was going around the neighbours selling small bundles of kindling. I hope this brings a vision of a young child trudging through snow in the woods carrying an axe and felling branches and stripping and trimming them to make kindling. That is not nearly as efficient as taking bunches of kindling from the bag my mother kept in the coal cellar. That venture was quickly curtailed when a neighbour turned me in to my mother.

My own first venture at 8 years old was when my father stocked Beatles wallpaper and gave me a couple of rolls. The wallpaper had 8 different images of the Beatles plus their autographs. I cut these out and sold them around my school for pennies.

My next school business venture came as I entered the last year of primary school. The tradition was to sell your used books to the year below and buy your next year's books from the year above. A perfect learning exercise on pricing, buying and selling, haggling and negotiation. Cash flow was favourable, and it was even possible to buy to resell to your peers. Funding was provided by parents which ensured a fast-moving profitable market. Boys stood in groups in the playground bartering energetically.

I remember enjoying this annual venture immensely, after my first few disastrous deals with the smarter experienced older sellers. I learnt to move fast, get on to the next deal and to resell to cover any poor decisions. The perfect business grounding. Did I reinvest my profits and build a million-dollar enterprise? No, I bought sweets and toys?

My next venture in my senior schooldays was when I found mushroom spore packs in a shop. I imagined a mushroom empire. I took on a partner whose parents had a shed. We insulated the walls with polystyrene tiles, again from my father. Are you spotting a trend? We sourced manure from the local stables. My friend tired of shovelling manure and his parents reclaimed their shed. The business never grew a single mushroom.

As I started university, I recognized that a business venture was required to supply hard needed cash. I went on holiday to Spain. The pub we drank in was called the Flying Haggis. The owner did a big trade in Flying Haggis T-shirts. I had never seen a pub T-shirt in Aberdeen, so my new venture was born.

I sourced the T-shirts from a local retailer, we found an art teacher who could do screen printing. We started with a publican who owned one of Aberdeen's oldest pubs, Ma Cameron's. He had an old engraving which made the perfect T-shirt logo.

These T-shirts sold well but there were a couple of drawbacks. The blank T-shirts were expensive, and the publican insisted that we do the selling in his pub. We spent lots of time, sitting in the pub which created high overhead costs, in beer.

Demand grew, and we were not always there. The owner relented, and bar staff did the sales. I went to the commercial library and searched the name on the T-shirt label to find the wholesale supplier. The wholesale costs were lower, increasing our margin. I went further up the supply chain and was eventually buying from the importer.

We found other customers by targeting clubs. Eventually an offshore catering company asked us to produce T-shirts and sweatshirts for them to sell on the oil platforms they were contracted on. This was a real business. Demand was very high, the oil workers had plenty of money and our profits ensured an excellent university life. Only the need to study for our final exams halted this lucrative enterprise.

I graduated in law with further studies in accountancy, economics and statistics. The first job I took was as a buyer for an oil service company. My entrepreneurial experience stood me well in this fast-moving job. Every order was a negotiation. I was placing hundreds of orders every week.

I then joined a law firm to complete my training. I loved buying and selling property which was the most lucrative business for the firm. I was charging substantial legal fees but being paid apprentice wages. I did learn and I was good at what I did.

I disliked that those who most needed my help were badly served by me. The property side of the business required speed of reaction and focus to succeed. This resulted in the slower moving areas of law being set aside. Family law and other things that were dumped on my plate, suffered.

I was interested in contracts and skilled at drafting and negotiating these so once qualified it made sense for me to join an oil company in their contracts department. I joined Shell.

The work was interesting, and my law degree gave me a sound foundation in this exciting and challenging field. Working generally unsupported except for an engineer on the technical side, I negotiated contracts initially for, helicopters, fixed wing aircraft, and supply boats.

I then moved to drilling rig hire. At the age of 26 I negotiated a three-year contract with two years of options. The whole deal was worth over £200 million. Every sentence, sometimes a single word can be worth a lot of money in a negotiation which lasted a few days.

Working in this way gave me both knowledge and confidence. I left Shell and became commercial manager for a diving company. Contracts and bidding were my responsibility. I enjoyed this experience as I was exposed to every aspect of the company including the impact of revenue and cost on our balance sheet. I took on marketing as well as commercial. We increased turnover from £8 Million to £26 Million in a couple of years. The business grew before eventually being bought out by a larger company.

I resigned and joined another marine company which I hated every minute of except for the overseas travelling. I had meetings in Moscow right up to ministerial level.

The oil price collapsed and left me unemployed. I joined Shell in Malaysia as a self-employed contractor. It became a further learning exercise living in a town surrounded by jungle with my wife and young daughter. I had a brilliant boss I enjoyed working with. We developed some of the most innovative incentivized contracts developed in the industry many of which became Shell global standards.

I returned to the UK and joined BP. At this time John Browne became head of BP Exploration. We went through a massive change process, an experience I loved and learnt more from this experience than anything else in my career.

BP at that time was a company in which you could make a noticeable personal contribution. My contribution was recognised and rewarded. I, introduced incentivized contracts and various other innovations, working at times as an internal consultant.

I worked on the leadership team for two of our gas assets. I transferred to Grangemouth to the huge petrochemical complex working simultaneously for BP Oil and BP Chemicals.

My area of procurement and warehousing became the pilot for merging the two sides of the complex into a single organisation. It was an enjoyable if difficult period working with clever generous people every day.

It was time to get my entrepreneurial spirit back in gear. In my spare time, I joined a multi-level marketing organisation as an independent distributor working with my wife to grow our business. This took me out of my comfort zone, eventually making business presentations to large audiences. I presented to seven thousand people at the Cardiff International Arena. This enterprise was not for me with limited opportunity for introducing personal innovations.

I agreed with BP that I would leave, and they would give me a three-year contract to support my successor and the leadership of my old department. Corporate Fundamentals my first limited company was born.

The BP contract gave me the space to establish other clients. I worked from an office in my garage. My business model was to work two Client facing days a week. The breakthrough was getting subcontracted to deliver a course in the Middle East. I enjoyed working there. Abu Dhabi was lovely. I had lots of knowledge to contribute as the clients were oil companies and I loved the Emerati people.

After a period, I combined my company with a friend's company that did the same type of work all over the world. We built the business successfully for three years. Our clients were global blue-chip companies. This took me to Australia, Singapore, Azerbaijan, the Middle East, Europe and often to the USA from Houston to Alaska, Boston to Washington State. In the end, we had a difference of opinion and split into our own separate businesses again.

I went back to my own company contracting in the Middle East with the same clients. I also had work with a lubricants company which spanned the UK, US and the Far East. I really enjoyed working frequently with their leadership teams.

One of my Middle East clients requested I join a young management consultancy firm to support one of the oil company's senior leaders. I was reluctant but I lived 2 years permanently in Abu Dhabi which we loved. I became much more knowledgeable about management consultancy. During this period with change training programmes. I also supported an international oil company travelling back and forwards around the world.

When my Middle East work ended, I was offered the job of Senior Partner Oil and Gas Russia in a well-known international management consultancy. I became unwell so declined this opportunity. After some medical confusion, I was diagnosed with cancer in the form of Hodgkin's Lymphoma. During the treatment I suffered a severe stroke, which left me disabled.

I re-established my own company. I won a contract to reorganize the Abu Dhabi Education Council's contracts and purchasing organisation. This was a $2+ Million contact which I ran from the UK with periodic visits. I had a team of consultants in country, and it mostly went well but the work was exhausting, and it was clear I ought to retire.

I did retire but managed to write and co-author a few books. The Performance Connection with Dennis DeWilde Transformational Meetings and then this book with another two in progress.

I miss my business life every day, but I am thankful for the experiences good and bad, exciting and stressful.

Structure

The objective of this book is to help new and not-so-new businesses address the commercial processes which they may be unfamiliar with. It is a combination of information, examples, real world anecdotes and personal stories.

Section One - The Heart of your Business, covers your business idea and the need that it meets. It covers the vital emotional link that you have with your business and your market. In many ways this is the core of your idea and energy to power you towards your Goals.

Section Two - Getting Started, describes choosing a name, finding a business idea, legal frameworks, the process of change from employment to self-employment and ensuring that it is the right business for you.

Section Three - Business Planning: Creating the business plan, defining your objectives, setting your strategy and monitoring and analysing your progress.

Section Four - Marketing and Sales: Sales planning, customers, engagement and the 6 S's, product, people, place, price, promotion and positioning as well as considerations of competition.

Section Five - Operations and Administration: Commercial arrangements in your work. Including scoping work, estimating and tendering for projects. Scheduling the work, concluding contracts, executing the work.

Section Six - Finance: Budgeting, forecasting and monitoring work over the financial period.

Section One - The Heart of your Business

Pitfalls

This marks the start of the Pitfalls I identified as being the main obstacles to business success.

'The root of business failure rarely lies with actions taken but rather in your omissions'

Pitfall 1 - The Absence of Need

The most successful products and services identify and meet a need. Sometimes, identifying a need that nobody realized they had up to that time.

Identify a burning need and uncover opportunity no matter how basic the product is. Someone invented the match for which there was, indeed, a burning need.

Many products and services are created for their inventor's self-satisfaction. Products for which there is no need. They do not succeed.

Not every business idea will work, even well-resourced ones, with loyal clients and products. Many business ideas fail for the best organizations.

The need might be in how a product is delivered or packaged not necessarily the product itself. Think of EasyJet for example. Low cost, safe convenient travel was a new approach to air travel. This new approach was EasyJet's USP. (Unique Selling Point). A great USP defines how a customer need is met.

Your Deeper Purpose

Your business at its heart may offer more than its obvious product. I had a local butcher once who offered more than high quality meat. He was a hub for the community, supporting every charity and local community initiative. His true purpose could have been summarized as:

Nourishing the community with quality meats and community support.

I worked with a fantastic young lady entrepreneur. She provided excellent online teaching lessons, planning and learning resources for primary-one pupils. Her well-conceived products were much more to her clients than resources. Her deeper product was:

Support teachers by optimizing their time planning and resourcing superior learning.

Giving back time to busy teachers was her most valuable product and what she was known and appreciated for providing.

A deeper Purpose anchors your business in a more successful place.

Pitfall 2 - An idea out of Time

Now is probably a bad time to be in the abacus business. CD's had their day with the advent of online streaming and downloads, yet bizarrely vinyl disks are making a comeback when it seemed their time was over.

The often-repeated business idea that didn't succeed was the Sinclair C5. The predecessor of electric vehicles.

The C5 suffered from undeveloped technology in batteries with limited range, looked ungainly and became a bit of a joke. The idea of a personal electric vehicle now is right at the forefront of technology as battery power increased and renewables are forcing petrol and diesel cars off the road.

The Sinclair C5 is making a comeback in a modified form. Electric bikes and scooters are also set to become huge sellers.

Identify the business cycle, when assessing the viability of a business idea. Is your idea novel and sustainable or a fad? Will the business stand the test of time?

Is the idea dependent on other technologies which are changing or being replaced? Will emerging technologies and products replace your idea? What is happening in the world that will impact your idea?

If the idea succeeds will others move to copy it? These things

must be considered for long-term success.

Innovation and being first in a market will only succeed if the idea can be protected. Search around, you may already be a late entrant to the market.

New products always present challenges. In many ways this is why existing products and services done in new and better ways present larger opportunities.

Who would imagine that the world needed Facebook, Twitter, You Tube or Amazon or an iPhone, yet these became multi-billion-dollar businesses? What will you imagine and create?

Pitfall 3 - An Idea that misses the Business Cycle

In times of war, holidays and beachwear are not successful sellers. Commodities, industrial staples and arms sell well.

Now is not the best time for starting a coal mining business. Mining lithium is quite another matter, which might mean reopening the old Cornish tin mines where Lithium is abundant.

Coal mining at one time was the recipe for colossal success. The world moved on. Renewables is a theme even beyond its infancy; many companies are now well established. New technologies like quantum computing are in their earliest stages but those who risked money on research and development and establishing the technologies will reap the rewards.

Things are in demand sometimes and at times they are not. People tend not to spend when money is in short supply. If you are selling luxury goods be aware of consumer trends, yet essentials are always required no matter what the circumstances. Food and funerals will always be in demand.

Some businesses buck these trends. In buoyant times alcohol sales are high. In bad times alcohol sales are also strong but for different reasons.

Be aware of the right business and business cycle issues. Keep your eyes up and constantly monitor your business situation.

Pitfall 4 - Failure to Establish Brand

Every area of business has competitors. Your brand makes you distinctive. Brand is what you most relate to in your business and which attracts customer loyalty. Brand attracts customers and enlists then as your supporter. Brand may be subtle, how you service your customers or thank them for their custom. Brand need not be expensive and bold. The absence of brand results in a lack of distinctiveness.

Brand Questions

Who is the target market? (Describe this as a single person.)

Age

Gender

Employment

Hobbies

Education

Lifestyle

Personas

Develop 3-6 sets of descriptions of individual who meet these criteria. Picture them exactly to identify who your business is delivered to and how they might react to your strategy.

Give them names. When you develop a marketing idea or product variant imagine how this will appear to each of our personas.

What service do I provide?

What is the need your business meets? What problem does your business solve? In what ways do your customers appreciate what you do, how you do it and how do you meet their requirements?

What is the magic?

What makes your business sparkle? What delivers the wow factor that customers love and tell their friends about? What emotional attachment is created in them?

Why me?

What do you uniquely bring to your business that others do not bring as well, often or individually?

What Image do I want to portray?

Image is a desirable thing and its distinguishing features. Image describes the public face of your business to its customers and separately how the business feels to your staff, subcontractors and insiders. How does that image resonate with your customers?

What am I passionate about that provides the energy to help me through?

Find your passion. Passion is the core of how your business appears to your customers and how you feel about your work. Passion transcends bad days, problems and challenges. It is the strongest connection between you and your business. The saying, you are not your job. is true but your work ought to be your passion.

When I worked with Castrol a brilliant business full of dedicated people, they had identified a customer category they described as *Passionates.*

These individuals were passionate about the vehicles they owned, mainly cars and motor bikes. They wanted the best lubricants to look after these treasured vehicles.

The Castrol teams were equally dedicated to producing these products and passionate about meeting their customer needs. Many were Passionates themselves which the car park bore testament to!

What gets me up each morning anxious to rush to work to deliver?

This is a method for finding your passion. When I am truly passionate about a project, I wake up early with ideas to move forward on, I start working on them promptly and produce exceptional work. Everybody recognizes me for this passion which I become strongly identified with. Whatever problems arise, Passion helps me to push through. If you find your single passion and something that remains your passion for at least 3 years you will succeed.

Your brand in 4 words:

Take some time to this. What words encapsulate your brand? Share these with your customers, family and friends. Do they say? 'Yes, that is your business, that is you, perfect'. Would they suggest more appropriate words?

To arrive at your brand use these questions to develop your thinking. I usually reduce these to a brand statement based on 3-5 single words with a paragraph expanding on each.

Pitfall 5 A Lack of Excitement

Running your own business whilst enjoying independence and the opportunity to prosper is not easy. I would not wish to discourage anyone but there are times when it is hard, frustrating, demoralizing and downright depressing. When life and business seem unfair. To succeed keep going.

Do something you love, enjoy and are excited about. The latest fad or whim just won't keep you going through the tough times.

The time to get things right is at the beginning. You will waste time on false starts, rethinks or new ideas if you fail to take the time to select the right subject business for you from the start.

I love business, but that does not mean that any business will do. I confess I analysed dozens maybe hundreds of business ideas. Almost all short-lived, excuses to spend money or just not rewarding enough to get me past the first three months before my interest shifts, I have doubts, or I get bored. Can I sustain this interest and work consistently for at least three years is a good test of any business idea?

After three years you will make it successful if it has the potential. You might in that time develop a version of it that has more potential and develop that as you proceed.

A successful business often emerges from a business which is worked to the stage of being the launch pad for a more successful version. This point might have never been reached without starting and persevering with its original version.

One such business that springs to mind was Virgin. It started as a chain of small music and clothes shops run by a very young entrepreneur. Anyone who visited this shop could not have envisaged the vast modern outlets it now operates globally far less the wider Virgin organisation with an airline, railways, megastores, music, banking, space travel, media and so much more. If Richard Branson had grown bored with the retail business and moved straight to the holiday company the group might not be what it is today.

Start, work hard, keep going with a single focus on the one business to the exclusion of all other business ideas.

Section Two Getting Started

Pitfall 6 - Choosing the wrong Business

Many entrepreneurs are looking for guaranteed success in a business idea or following a whim. This section focuses on how to think about what business you should start. If you are unable or unwilling to do this thinking, then perhaps self-employment is not for you. Many entrepreneurs chose the wrong business for them or fail to notice factors which by taking a slightly different approach would have produced a much better result.

The business idea is important however not the only success factor. We look around and admire those ideas that have made their creators successful.

If only we thought of the next major hit and have the technical ability to create such a product. We might possess the management expertise to employ those who would develop this for us.

There is an important distinction. Will you be the business or manage the business?

Business ideas tend to come in waves. Remember the so-called dot com bubble, where online businesses thrived seemingly to the detriment of all others. However, look around you at people who are being successful. Some of their business fields will have existed for thousands of years. Joiners, butchers, undertakers, food retailers, tailors to name some of these. People will always need food, clothing and a myriad of services and goods to live their lives. An idea does not always have to be new or novel to be successful.

"How do I come up with a business idea that I can follow?

The Matrix

The matrix is a tool I have used for myself and for others looking to identify opportunities.

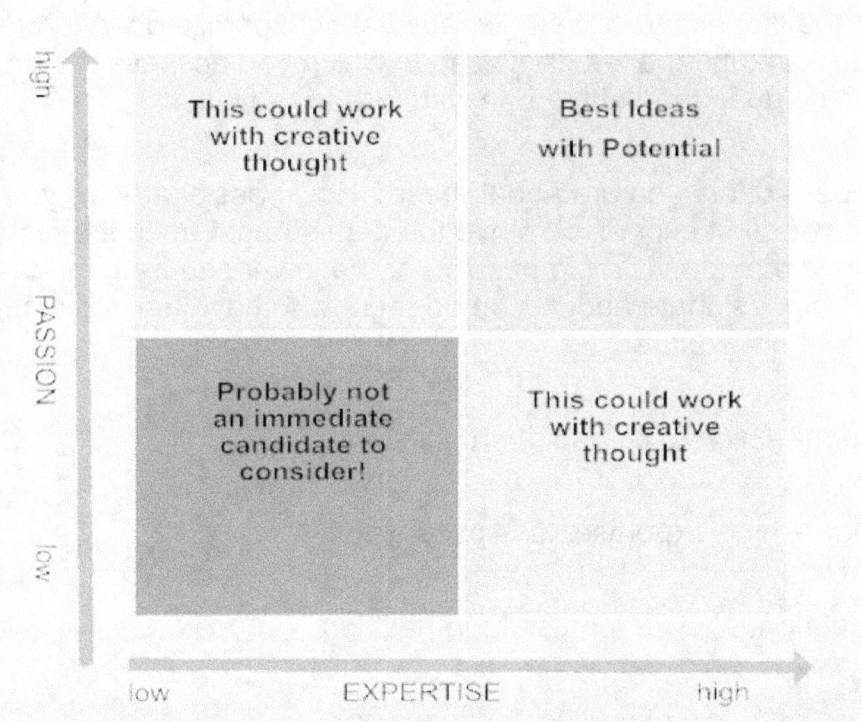

Take a large piece of paper or whiteboard. Draw a square covering most of the paper. The line along the lower edge (if you paid attention at school you will know this as the x-axis) we will title Expertise. The line up the left side (the y Axis) we title Passion. Draw a line from the middle of the x-axis vertically up to the top of the square. Draw another from the middle of the y-axis horizontally across the square. You should now have a square divided into 4 equal smaller squares resembling the example above.

Take another piece of paper and brainstorm a list of the areas that you have expertise, skills and knowledge in. Writing each of these on sticky notes works best.

Do a realistic assessment on two counts. First, what *saleable* expertise do you have. Second, what activities are you capable at or willing to become capable at doing? Write everything down and more, committing you to nothing yet.

Take the first expertise item; what level of expertise do you have? Place this along the x-axis. Those in which you possess the most expertise go to the right, those with less to the left.

How passionate you are about these? How passionate are you about your first expertise? Move the idea straight up to the highest square if that idea is a big passion or the lower square for ideas you are less passionate about. You ought now to have ideas distributed among the 4 squares:

Top right – high expertise, high passion

Top left – high expertise, less passion

Bottom right – low expertise high passion

Bottom left – low expertise, low passion

Some areas we are expert in, some things get us less excited about. We are screening these as business ideas. Your most likely business opportunities lie in the top right square. Doing something you have expertise in and are passionate about is most likely to be a great candidate to build a business on.

Don't neglect the other topics. If you look at those topics you are most passionate about might you acquire the expertise needed to succeed. In the top left square what would need to be different for you to become passionate about the things you have high expertise but lower passion about.

Think what it might take to develop the idea in a way which you can increase your expertise. Perhaps, focus on a specific niche where your expertise is high, or you have specific interest or passion.

How can you find a way to shape the opportunity so that your idea moves towards the top right square? Anything in the bottom left area is unlikely to be promoted although be thoughtful about why you came up with the idea anyway.

Look first at the top right square. These are ideas you have expertise and passion in are the things you are most likely to succeed in and stick at when things become tough. What would this idea look like as a business?

Think laterally, for example you might be expert at cattle breeding and have a passion for breeding. This might suggest a business farming livestock. Developing a business in artificial insemination might be an option or exporting livestock or meat, you might become a breeding or blood line consultant or provide farmers with software recording livestock bloodlines.

Keep going with this process until you have a long list of possibilities.

Take the time to think of 4 or 5 great businesses from this exercise. Think for a while, what is getting you excited. Which business might get you out of bed early and happy every day?

Is the idea something you have always been interested and expert or is this just a very recent notion. We all have these and fall into this trap. Do not build a business on a passing notion or a fad. Is this an idea that will be around in ten years' time?

Develop a list of options which you can research, evaluate, discuss and ultimately make a choice on. Plant the seeds in your mind and nurture those that grow.

A start up business from your job

I started my first substantial business in this way. I had expertise in procurement and contracts and had a passion around meeting facilitation. I told my employer I was planning to leave and asked them if there was a way to continue to support them once I left. I departed with a three-year contract to consult with my successor and his team. This gave me a start, kept me in the loop with a big organisation and guaranteed me income for three years.

I identified an opportunity to deliver a training course in Procurement. From this contact developed a couple of large consulting opportunities as a subcontractor to a larger consultancy. The work was on a major restructuring in Abu Dhabi where I consulted on the contracts and purchasing areas and on meeting facilitation and change. Once established with this client I spotted or created new work opportunities with them.

Over the next few years procurement decreased as part of my business until I was doing none of it. Ten years later I won a large procurement consultancy contract worth over $2 million - you never know!

An important take away from this is your business will develop over time. You may well find yourself doing different things for different clients than you imagined at the start.

I had to get started to be 'in the game' and find the opportunities to move my business forward.

A start up business from your hobby

Many people develop businesses out of their hobbies. You are interested in tropical fish. Options available to you might include:

Obvious ideas such as, opening a tropical fish supplies shop or to breed tropical fish and supply small pet shops

Less obvious ideas such as - building and installing fish tanks

Obscure but innovative ideas including – to design, stock and maintain fish tanks for company receptions.

Do not be restricted by your immediate thoughts.

Brainstorm, just like I did above, keep throwing out different ideas until you run out of ideas. Keep going, the next few thoughts may take a while to emerge, but they will be crackers. 'This is your subconscious at work - a process called the 'learning edge' which you can learn to harness to your benefit.

Start-up businesses grown from other's ideas

Take ideas that others have and using them, adapting them or reframing them. existing business ideas can be more difficult, you have to be wary of breaches of copyright etc.

Be alert to ideas you can replicate or improve. Travels abroad are great sources of ideas. I was on holiday in Venice once and the memory card in my camera soon filled up. A camera shop had the idea of putting customers photos on a CD-ROM, so I cleared my memory card and was able to start again. I noticed they were selling CD's of photos taken in Venice at different times of year. I could not have taken these shots, but this got me thinking. This suggested two potential business ideas:

Scotland is a huge tourist destination. Take pictures of the main cities, major events and inaccessible locations. Sell CD's with photographs through vending machines at the main travel hubs airports, rail stations and at the service stations on the motorway. Sell video on DVD using the same vending machines.

How you think about business and how energetically you implement the idea are important.

Start a business by doing things better

Your expertise or interests may lie in an area that is attracting many businesses. This should not put you off, indeed you should be reassured that businesses are successful through this approach. Modify the approach to give yourself a successful niche by doing things better?

Take a joinery business for example what are the key problems from the customer's perspective now? A problem creates a need.

Imagine, you think they are:

· Co-ordinating different trades

· Getting convenient dates

· Co-ordinating delivery for the job when customers buy their own materials.

· Getting competitive prices for items to be fitted by a joiner

· Customers ability to be present during working hours

I made these up but think how you might develop a more unique service around these:

Co-ordinate all the trades required to complete the job. Target a young business market using the web or smart phone apps to optimize bookings on convenient days. Use your access to trade prices to purchase the components for your clients. Do more work at unsocial hours for yourself say weekends, holidays and evenings. Now brainstorm more problems and customize your offering with smart solutions.

How would this apply to your ideas?

What about the different problems' joiners face, list these and look for win: win solutions to improve your business model?

Say these are:

- Keeping a constant flow of work

- Getting paid promptly

Could you provide:

special offers for people willing to have work done when the time is most suitable to you by providing them a discount?

Give discounts for upfront payments?

Set up a joinery booking system online for a group of self-employed joiners so capitalizing on changes of technology.

You might have to provide some form of guarantee of delivery. Be creative, speak to your bank about Bank Guarantees?

Ask customers about you provide financing for their project, what opportunities might that open up?

Start a business by doing things differently

A potential approach is to take an established business model and to approach it differently. Combine your idea with problems that exist for others. Is there a need to fill or a problem to solve.?

In this example let's take a coffee shop. You have worked in a well-known chain, you know how the business operates, enjoy the business and are passionate about providing convenient, high quality coffee to customers.

The conventional franchised coffee shop approach is expensive.

Many small commuter-towns lack coffee shops where the established coffee drinker can access to their daily brew.

Perhaps you start a van-based coffee business taking the coffee to the consumer rather than the opposite.

Now here's another angle by combine two problems to create an opportunity.

The second problem is the absence of employment opportunities.

Create a coffee van franchise giving others the opportunity to rent a van, buy their consumables and vend coffee.

Combine this with the issue of stay-at-home mums looking for employment.

What about creating a mom-and-pop franchise where you rent a coffee machine and sell consumables. Provide marketing help to individuals living in smaller locations who can open up their kitchen and provide a table for coffee or a carry out service during certain hours of the day to generate a small but steady income. There will be food hygiene legislation issues here so solve them and the best of luck to you.

More people working from home is a growing trend which makes such ideas more viable.

Look at different delivery mechanisms for any idea that you have.

Let's look at a Butchery business as an example.

Different delivery

Take orders online and deliver in chilled insulated container or provide a van-based service?

Different products

Focus on more exotic meats buffalo, venison, kangaroo, goose, rare breed pork, chickens, etc?

Specialize on the entire supply chain, farm to butchery for a single type of meat.

Different sourcing

Bring in meats from abroad?

Different marketing

Create relationships with specialist farmers to create a unique branding of your products?

Make extensive use of social media to promote sales at markets. Start a butchery blog with articles about new and special cuts, the use of less well-known cuts and associated suppliers?

Combine promoting your products with diet and nutritional advice, recipes, or some other ideas?

Different location

Family butchers have largely disappeared, and their personal touch has gone in favour of supermarkets. Can you use social media to create a dialogue with a community of customers to reinvent that relationship?

By combining all these ideas, identify and solve problems in the market and meet that need. A very conventional business would be changed into a unique, thriving contemporary business idea.

You can do this for any business idea you have.

Start Up Business Ideas Spoiled for Choice

You will now with some effort have generated six wonderful ideas that you are interested in and excited about getting started with. Now chose your best option, this is always a difficult moment. Every choice means eliminating some ideas you have invested in albeit only emotionally.

You will need to do some research to properly define and specify what the idea really is and what its pros and cons are before deciding.

A shortcut is to put a flip chart sized piece of paper up on the wall in your home for each idea with two columns titled pros and cons. Write up those pros and cons that spring to mind and keep adding thoughts as they occur. Keep this on the wall for a month or so, add more pros and cons as they occur to you. This is important enough to take plenty of time over.

You might want to be more scientific and create a spreadsheet with a set of categories against which your ideas can be compared. Profit potential, saleability, capital required, ease of start-up, customer potential, competition, running costs would be your column headings.

You would have to identify your own categories based on your needs and your business knowledge, comfort zone or anything else that arises.

Based on my categories here is a short explanation:

Profit potential what is your view of the opportunity to buy low and sell high? Or to what extent will your idea have a niche market allowing you to charge more for your services?

Saleability One day you might want to sell your business? The key to saleability is whether somebody else after purchasing can operate using your business model and processes is able makes the same or more profit?

Capital required if you are self-funding or starting with loans the less the start-up cost the more advantageous.

Ease of start-up Why not start a small? Test the market and grow later? Perhaps while still working a job?

Customer potential Do some market research to test how to identify, target and secure business? Are your customers readily identified and easily contacted?

Competition Do large number of competitors exist in your given market with advantages over your idea?

Running costs How significant will your running costs be including your own requirements. How rapidly will your business move into profit?

Now score each of these items for each idea. Choice is an emotional not an intellectual exercise. Be objective as you make your choice. We cheat our own ranking systems. Every idea has 'cons'z so don't underestimate these.

Pitfall 7 - An inappropriate Legal Structure

I do not intend to make this a small company law book but there are legal topics I will address in outline. The legal structure of your business is an important consideration. Your lawyer or accountant and local business advice organisation can advise you on issues of liability, taxation rules, risk exposure and company regulations and returns to make this a significant decision. You can start with one structure and change in the future. Each structure has different consequences, costs, benefits and obligations. Each choice has significant consequences.

Sole Trader

The most common business is one that is only you. Over a million such businesses exist in the UK.

There is no limit to your liability for loss, injury or death. The only limit is your personal financial limits beyond which you would have to declare bankruptcy. Many people don't imagine this is a big issue. If you lose your house, car, other assets, all your money and a lot more besides, this might change your thinking. A personal bankruptcy is a devastating experience. Your profits are taxable and require to be declared. Your business expenses are deductible in most cases and these need careful record keeping.

Partnership

A Partnership is a business with two or more partners who are the owners. A partnership creates what is called, joint and several liability. This means every partner is liable.

Joint liability is created between the partners but if any single partner cannot pay from money and assets the liability continues to those who can pay, until the liability is met.

Partnerships are governed by a partnership agreement, describing the rights, obligations and processes between the partners. Partnerships are common in professional firms such as Accountants, Lawyers, Architects etc.

Limited Liability Partnerships

More common now are limited liability partnerships, but I will not delve into these. If you consider this format as a possibility you will need legal advice.

Limited Company

The most common legal structure for a company is the Limited Company. Shareholders of the company bear the risk to the limit of their shareholding comprised by the total assets of the company.

Limited Companies provide good protection and are preferred by many larger clients but the come with rules about accounting and tax and company returns. They have higher start up and annual costs. If your business is a limited company, the company is a separate legal entity from yourself. You are an employee. You pay Income tax and tax on any dividends. The company pays Corporation Tax. If the company goes bankrupt your own assets are protected unless you as a Director have behaved fraudulently.

Others

A variety of other less common business structures are available which a lawyer can advise you on.

Pitfall 8 - A Bad Business Name

The choice of name is important when you start your business. A name is so easy to rush into in the excitement of getting started. A key piece of advice here. Stop and think a lot.

Legal restrictions arise around company names. You will invest money and energy in your name, and this will be the foundation of your brand.

Let me share a story with you. We named one of my businesses Meetings that Work. The business ran and facilitated meetings. This catchy name seemed a great choice. We paid for design, stationery and website, domains and more. We checked the name was legal and not used by other businesses. We chose it from a short list of 20 or, so we generated.

All was fine, until at our first Christmas night out when one of our female staff came back from the toilets laughing. She had met someone from another company at the same event. Seeing the fun, we were having and the cross-section of ages of men and women she noticed the company name on the table plan and assumed we were a dating company of some description.

This connection had never occurred to us but once pointed out, the potential confusion was obvious. We decided to change our name and rebranded at considerable cost. Not the tens of millions multi-nationals pay of course but still money we would have liked to avoid paying. We did have other reasons at that time to contemplate rebranding.

This was not my only messed up business name. I launched an online meeting blog I had intended to monetize. Traffic was good but visitors were struggling to get my emails and were sometimes blocked from the site. The site name was *themeetingsexpert*. Do you see an issue? Some content blockers spotted the word *sex* in the name. Embarrassing!

The first piece of advice I was given was not to use your own name. Nothing is wrong with using your own name, but careful thought on the longer term is required. Is your name your brand? Your own name still needs checking. For example, an outdoor clothing business uses my name as its brand. Names are very far from unique look yours up on Facebook. Well over 200 Geoff Andersons appear only two of which profiles are mine. We are not as unique as we might like to believe.

Brainstorm a list of names, in the UK check Companies House to find if the name or something very close to it, is taken.

Look at domain names is yours available? Even if so, search the name in a browser for what turns up.

Names can be illegal or restricted in some countries. For example, in the UK and most other countries rules prevent, using the same or similar name of another company without permission: The Marks and Spencer would not be permitted!

Sensitive names include the use of British, institute, Tribunal or a name which implies pre-eminence or includes a word that implies a regulated activity - bank, government or local authority. The use of offensive names is not permitted. The use of certain characters or symbols is not permitted. The use the term ltd. or limited has rules about use. Web addresses do not permit symbols. I once wanted to use '&' but this is forbidden as are other symbols.

Regulations vary by the type of company structure - limited company, partnership, plc. Professions have their rules as well. The government website gives lots of guidance. Being a Sole Trader does not necessarily exclude you from the regulations, if the name is designed to confuse to attract business.

In the US: Many of the same rules apply. Check for trademarks, check for identical or similar names and as get advice from a qualified professional.

Now some general advice for choosing your company name:

Think how your chosen name will look on a logo. Search Google for 'odd looking logos' for some cracking examples – over 18s only! What connotations does your name create for example the 'MissMellie cake company' would not be a good choice unless you spotted a market gap in particularly malodorous cakes. Ensure your name is unique and memorable for the right reasons.

Avoid odd spellings, they confuse customers and are often entered wrongly in web searches.

Be as simple as you can. This has become progressively more difficult. To get an original name using simple common words now means that only a compound of two words will give you uniqueness. This is most noticeable when creating web domains. Choose a name with some logical connection to your chosen field. Neither too formal nor informal depending on your market.

Ensure there is opportunity for future growth or expansion.

An amusing name might suit your current brand and clients but if things go well larger clients and official bodies might not share your sense of humour.

If you can, Register the name. Claim domains, and social media names. If you intend to grow a larger business secure the .com, .co.uk, .co. .org and .net and those for specific industries if the industry or geographic suffix e.g. .scot or .photo exist. You can spend a great deal of money securing every variable available .uk is now a suffix but this explosion of alternative suffixes will never end so focus on the main ones. Providers sell packages of names, low cost in early years but increasing in later periods.

Before committing, live with the name for a while and test the name on others.

Names can be changed in future but once you have built business, contacts and branding a change is costly. Better to take time and effort and to make a good choice first which you can live with for years.

By sticking with a domain name for a long period your website ranking improves.

A client of mine has a design business. Over the space of 5 years, they have been (wrongly) threatened with expensive legal action over a trading name, a case they would have won but at unaffordable cost. They rebranded again as the next name became someone else trademark! Name 3 they chose was the two owners names until they went their separate ways.

The remaining partner replaced this a great trendy name which worked well at that time. As I write they have rebranded again having moved into a different market requiring a more professional name.

I have often made bad choices which I lived to regret, changing a few times before I settle on a great name. Take the time to select a great name, a name you can be proud of as your business grows.

Now build your Brand around that name.

Pitfall 9 - Maintaining an Employee Mentality

The move from paid employment to self-employment is difficult for anyone without any type of business background in their family. Self-Employment is a different lifestyle. Your future is in your own hands and you also get to enjoy the benefits. A failure to escape the employee mentality can be fatal.

Employees get guaranteed income (sometimes not always), you get your job and work managed by others. HR calculate your salary and tax and pension. Your boss supervises your work and your outcomes and productivity.

All these things now become your responsibility. You don't get the luxury of putting things off, nor of taking 'duvet days'. Productivity is up to you, every day. You suffer the consequences If you let things slip.

Lesson One: You are entitled to nothing. Holidays, labour rights, welfare payments. If something to be done on Christmas Day only you can do it. Your triumphs are your making and so are your disasters.

If you have employees, they become your responsibility. There will be frustrations and disappointments as you recognise that they too have an employee mentality. That is their right. It is why, you get the benefits of self-employment, and they do not although many imagine they ought to. There is a line to lay down until they are prepared to share in the risk obligations and responsibilities.

One way to make the transition and have any employee traits pointed out is to get yourself a Mentor. A Mentor can share their own experience of doing the things that you want to do. A Mentor can hold you accountable for following through on the things you both identified as needing done. This might sound like employing a boss. It is not, as either of you can terminate a mentoring relationship at any time. You can ignore mentor's advice, at your own risk.

No one owes you anything you make your own future. Be independent. Take responsibility.

Pitfall 10 The Wrong Business Partners

When you launch a new Business, it is not uncommon to invite business partners to join you. It is reassuring to have someone to discuss issues with, to share problems and successes. My experience is that partnerships are fraught with problems and by choice ought to be avoided. A business partner can be reassuring when taking a step into the unknown.

Some partners join in for the wrong reasons. Perhaps they fear the business will succeed big time, and they missed out. Perhaps joining in a new company is simpler than getting a job. Do they want to be in business but not be prepared to start a business by themselves?

I had a business partner who once we launched our business was scared of making phone calls!

My son had a business partner who joined so that his parents would stop nagging him to get a job. His friend's first policy was the business ought to pay for everyone's lunch.

Another of his partners took on the administrative duties but put all the bills and official paperwork into a drawer and failed to deal with them.

Neither I nor my son were innocent parties in all these failings.

I wanted support from someone.

He wanted capital.

I was the bad partner once. The expectation at that time was that I would do the sales. I did eventually become good at sales even cold calling but at that stage I lacked good skills. My business partner was an over-spender. An over-spender and an under seller are a stressful partnership all round. To be fair, I did generate large sales but through existing customers who enjoyed working with me but not my partner. This did not leave me time to market to others.

If partners are to be contemplated remember that whilst resources are doubled, so are salaries. Any and every business partner is an overhead unless they can perform the work well or sell the work well.

Partners are all about motivation.

What are your motivations in inviting partners to join your venture?

What are the partners motivations in wanting to join?

Does your businesses success need the skills your potential partner brings? Is employing someone with more skills an economic option?

If you were advertising the position would your potential partner be the preferred applicant?

Could you manage without the partner by getting advice from others without any long-term commitment?

A bad decision in choosing the wrong one can have horrible consequences, financially and emotionally, to you and your business. You might lose a friend, both of you will have stories. In one case I am familiar with, a former business partner took to the internet and libelled the individual and his business so that lawyers had to become involved.

Partnerships often succeed. Partnerships are never equal. One always works more than the other or is liked more by certain clients or respected more by the staff. Petty jealousy goes deep in these unequal partnerships. In big Partnerships there can be different types of partners with different ownership right and different earnings.

Even in these large firms the differences cause issues and stress. The two senior partners owned the offices. It was their hope that on retirement the younger partners would purchase the offices from them, to fund their retirement. The younger partners preferred to leave and start elsewhere in more suitable partnerships or on their own.

I never in my life felt worse than when one of my business partnerships went wrong. The dispute was resolved but I suspect to neither of our satisfaction. We both lost out in the end. The roots of the dispute ran deep, back to the launching of the business.

Be even more diligent about taking on Business Partners than you would about employing staff.

Pitfall 11 A Reluctance to Learn

Having knowledge about the business you are launching is undoubtedly helpful. Many successful businesses are based on exceptional knowledge and a high level of previous experience of the chosen business field.

Knowledge can be gained, and skills learnt. Conversely, individual have entered new fields with new thinking and made billions.

A lack of knowledge without a dedication to learning inevitably leads to problems. The single biggest cause of failure through a lack of knowledge is by those *not knowing what they don't know.* In any new field you enter into, a period of time learning with an existing business is worth considering. You might offer to work there unpaid, anything to accumulate insights.

A lack of knowledge leaves you open to being unable to complete work that you have won or worse facing legal challenge for incompetence. The biggest risk for those who sell well and speak a good game is that due to their lack of competence they fail to deliver the work they win. Those who succeed on limited knowledge learned fast, employed knowledgeable staff, and worked hard.

Even for those who are well trained, skilled and experienced in the work, a lack of business knowledge, acumen and skills can be equally dangerous. I have seen too many businesses where the owner was skilled in the work but failed due to lacking the necessary other business skills.

Few business opportunities don't need an element of learning before kicking off.

I know of one business which launched with limited skills and can now proudly state that they are world-class in their chosen area. This required constant study and practice and a willingness to be a student of their business. A level of dedication I admire.

These days many ways to learn are available.

You can learn online from free or paid video course, even attending courses from prestigious American Universities on You Tube free of charge. Books exist on everything as well as conventional training course.

Anybody can set themselves up as an online trainer. Too many of these tutor's knowledge is limited or flawed.

A useful rule is only to take advice from those who have achieved demonstrable success. Only, if an author has written a best-seller is their book about writing a best-seller worth buying. The same principle in financial markets might be only to take financial advice from those more successful with money than you are.

You don't need to know everything about your chosen field.

Lifelong learning should be a commitment which goes along with a commitment to pursue your ideas. Successful executives are rumoured read an average of two books a month. I have no reason to dispute this and every successful businessperson I know reads a great deal about their chosen field and a lot more besides.

Learners also mix with experts in their field to learn from others. I continue to read at least three books a month. A friend of mine subscribes to a service which summarizes the key points from several books a month, a useful and productive alternative.

Different people have different learning styles. Some like to read; others like to listen or view tutorials some only learn by doing but that has its limitations. Identify your preferred learning style and access a suitable learning vehicle.

Planning, sales, operations and finance all intersect on completion of each job won. You will learn how effective your processes are at this point. Developing a successful business will depend on your ability to extract the maximum from each learning opportunity.

Every piece of work completed, or sale made or even lost provides a learning opportunity for you and your business. I emphasise the value of these learning opportunities. It is easy to forget a completed job in the rush to move on to the next.

Here is my ten-question checklist to complete after ever piece of work or major sale made.

1. Was a job well priced?

2. Did you omit anything from your pricing or scope?

3. Did you make the profit you anticipated?

4. Are you winning too much or too little work? Were you overpriced or under-priced?

5. Are you able to deliver the quality expected for your price?

6. How much contingency did you use?

7. Was the time and resources you estimated correct?

8. Could the job have been completed in a more efficient way?

9. How did suppliers and contractors perform?

10. What learning should be taken from this job into the future?

A useful additional question is:

Was there anything in the completed job that might be offered as product to other customers?

Take the example of building a stand-alone cupboard. Made first as a bespoke item. In future if you used the same design, bulk buy components, bulk cut parts and you offer the cabinet to a larger market.

I used this idea a lot and over the years it became a money maker. The work, time and cost sunk in designing training course I was able to use again by delivering the same course to other clients. This adds both to your client base and to your turnover and profits.

Learning is vital to business growth. Ask your customers if they were happy with your product or service. Would they use you again? Would they recommend you to friends? What would they like you to do differently or what other services would they like you to offer? Be open to all feedback. Feedback is worth money to you and by learning you improve in the future.

Pitfall 12 The Wrong Motivation

In deciding to become self-employed or start a new business I urge you to be honest with yourself about your motivation for doing so. Your motivations are your own. No criticism is intended I merely suggest that you be aware of what they are.

Being a Business Owner

I have met several new business owners who wanted the perceived kudos of being able to say, 'I own my own Business'. A perception that being self-employed somehow is more prestigious than being in employment exists in some quarters.

The modern world of work values innovation and entrepreneurial skills as much as the world of self-employment.

To be successful you will need to be hard-working, have a skill set and have ideas. You earn the right to tell family and friends you own your own business. Believe me the possibility of this is heavily outweighed by occasions where you might have to reveal failures even bankruptcy.

Owning a Business is never a motivation in itself. Working at something you love and are passionate about and enjoying serving your client, should be at the heart of your business.

Ending the nine to five

You will look back and laugh if this was your motivation. You will never work nine to five again. I don't think that many employees work none to five. I have worked 24-hour days.

I have sat up all night in hotel rooms writing reports on several occasions. I have woken up to write down thoughts that came into my mind. You will work evenings and weekends. In time this might become an enjoyable part of your life.

Of course, compensations are many. I did not take holidays for years; at times I flew my wife abroad when I was working to take a few days relaxing when the work was finished.

I would finish work early, enjoy a late lunch and a drink chilled white wine at the side of a pool in the sunshine, celebrating a job well done.

Weekends in the Middle East I went fishing in the Arabian Gulf. I visit new places, shopped in the souk and eat in great restaurants. Nothing comes free.

Not having a Boss

I was made redundant twice in my employed career. On two other occasions had worked for dreadful bosses. My main motivation was to be self-employed but in reality, I discovered that I was working for a different boss.

If not working for a boss meant doing what I wanted to, this was replaced by doing what I had to do. My client's expectations and my commitment to deliver on them became my new boss.

The discipline of reporting to a boss was replaced by the discipline of always doing what I said I would do or what was requested of me, every hour of every day.

Emails were replied to, bids and quotes done within 24 hours, invoices submitted immediately. Making every decision yourself regardless of how difficult and living with the consequences of those decisions. Not everyone can do this.

Making Lots of Money

High-profile wealthy people are seen to own their own business, which is perhaps why business is seen as the route to wealth and luxury. Some well-paid employed executives earn millions of pounds. Self-employment is not the only route to financial nirvana.

Although you control your own financial destiny many self-employed entrepreneurs earn much less than they would as employees. Think about this. Employment provides a salary, annual raises, promotions, pensions, bonuses, a company car, insurance and even share schemes and other perks. Replacing these requires building a profitable business.

Will you replace the perks of a job every year? I took ill later in my career and I certainly would have fared better for a period had I remained in employment. Nobody knows what the future holds.

'Turnover is Vanity Profit is Sanity'

Only the money that comes into your personal bank account is reality. You can easily fool yourself into thinking you are making a fortune, but turnover does not equate to profit.

Many businesses provide their owners a comfortable life. Many others just provide stress and minimal rewards. Your business must provide for you and your family every year. The pressure of finding and doing new work keeps going without fail.

My Businesses did give me and my family prosperity, a great home, lovely holidays in the later years. I spent money employment never provided, I visited places I would never have visited and indeed that was the biggest benefit of owning my own business.

I was lucky, and I was successful, but I might not have been.

Working from Home

Many new businesses are started from a desire to work from home, avoiding commutes or because circumstances like childcare oblige you to do this.

Many examples exist of successful home businesses. Home businesses face exactly the same challenges as any other plus the additional constraint of finding a suitable business that can work unrestricted from home. This is why so many 'authors' favour self-publishing.

The first thing I did when forced to retire was to write three books. I wrote from home; I still do, and I learnt to self-publish by buying a course online. I never made much money but enjoyed the experience and I was kept busy when I was recuperating. If you believe that writing might be a potential business for you, be aware that a good selling self-published book sells only 200 copies.

Home business can be run online these days and are well suited to that format. Home businesses that are successful can outgrow the home. The need to travel or visit clients or conferences becomes a part of your life defeating the initial home working plan. Even successful authors end up visiting publishers and doing book signings in bookshops

Section Three Business Planning

Business Planning Essentials

The following features are essential for every business irrespective of size. A small business or self-employed tradesman might create a less developed approach, still important, as the consequences of failure are much higher.

- Written Business Plan
- Objectives
- Strategy
- Research supporting the plan to deliver the Objectives

Business Plan

I cover preparing your Business Plan in detail later in this book. Spend time on this significant step in the process. By creating a plan on paper, you can improve your idea increasing its potential and testing, its viability, security and integrity.

Objectives

Objectives are the list of Goals you want your business to achieve. I love Objectives as they possess a real magic if well used.

Objectives are not a wish list, or an approximation of what you would like to achieve. Objectives are a target which is difficult enough to inspires you to come up with creative solutions. Once Objectives are written down it amazes me how the ways of achieving them appear.

When I worked for John Browne's BP, objectives were stretching. Once committed to, they become *promises* which had to be delivered. This gave energy, imagination and momentum to our activity. Use these to drive your business to much greater success.

Strategy

I wanted to set out the key strategic areas of Business Planning to clarify the essence of why you might think of these to substantially increase your profits and manage your risks.

This is not theory. My first business effort, the kindling venture had

Objectives: make money to buy sweets

A Business Plan: Package my mother's kindling into packs of ten sticks and sell them to neighbours for a few pence at the weekend

Strategy: Go to the ones who were home and most favourably disposed to me.

Marketing Plan: Go to Mrs. A first, ring the bell and tell her how good my kindling was to ask her to buy two bundles.

Strategy provides the answer to the questions: What, Where. When and Who, as well as Where not, When not, Where not and Who not. Strategy is a moving activity.

As the world your business operates in changes, strategy alters to meet that change. Strategy essentially prioritizes where you put your most effort and deploy your resources in the areas of *Product, Place, People, Price and Promotions* to outperform your *Competition*. Strategy is about choice. You cannot do everything, so Strategy articulates the choices you make and options you chose to eliminate. In a fast-moving world strategy is adapted to meet the situation in front of you.

Not all things can change. If you invested in new machinery or a building programme, this is a longer-term strategic decision which must be made to work, especially when the market changes. If your sales force is committed to sell a particular product to a particular market, that can be changed but with consequences.

The workforce and market can become confused and redeployment takes time to occur.

The military parallel is obvious. Wellington had canon, cavalry and infantry to deploy. He chose the ground on which they would fight. If a battle was going badly, he might be forced change his resource deployment. You can imagine the consequences of canon being moved elsewhere, cavalry swinging round to a different flank or infantry sprinting to a different formation. redeployment takes time and opportunities are lost in exchange for gaining new ones. Your business is the same.

Strategy is set against the business environment you are operating in. The method of initially mapping this business environment comes from your SWOT and PESTLE, these, form Sections in my suggested Business Plan format and more detail can be found in that section.

There are long term strategies the period of which depends on your business type. Substantial unchangeable decisions might be addressed in a 5 or 10-year strategy. For most Business their Business and Marketing plans may be 1 to 3-year strategies with are revisited no more than annually.

Research

The first step in the process is to find some reliable metrics on which to base your Business Plan. This is a vital step to enable you to:

Measure the extent of your potential market.

Estimate the sales you might generate from that market.

Arrive at an appropriate price for your product or service.

Determine the best approach to promotion to your chosen market.

Assess the level of competition in your market.

You can see that by finding these figures you can forecast the sales and hence the income your business might generate, and the time and resources needed to do that work. This also helps you to determine the size and expenses of trading that your business supports. The quality of your data and your assumptions will determine how confident you can be in your plan.

Sales forecasts are notoriously optimistic in new business plans. An example is the success of marketing efforts. The old 'rule of thumb' for Email or postal marketing was a success rate of 1-2%. Contact 2000 potential customers and you might win 10 - 20 sales. In many types of business this was an overestimate. your success rate depends on what industry you are in, the price of the item and how appropriate your audience is or in marketing terms how well qualified.

Qualification of prospects is the process of improving their chances of them buying from you. If they register an interest and ask for more information, they become more qualified as a prospective customer. Say you are selling new kitchens. An email list of people who meet the following criteria are a much better prospect and might indeed give you 2-5% results or better depending on data quality.

Own their own home.

Are remodelling their home.

Are interested in fitting a new kitchen.

Are able to afford your prices.

Now with the huge amounts of data that the social media companies hold, they can generate for you excellent prospects in targeted campaigns.

Pitfall 13 A Lack of Paper Planning

The Business Plan

The biggest mistake a new businessperson can make, in my mind is to fail to test ideas on paper. A Business Plan is the method to adequately create, monitor and test your idea.

I watch entrepreneurs pitch their idea on to TV programmes like Dragons Den only to be shown up for not understanding their own business. Some of them fail to spot obvious flaws, in their products, market, risks and finances. Many of them had already invested thousands of pounds in the idea, often money wasted.

Spend nothing until you test your business on paper. Paper or Digital files are cheap.

A well drafted high-level Business Plan is not a difficult thing to do, requiring a little time, a lot of through and smart research. What do you need to know? How can you find that out? You can create and develop your plan over a week or two. If your plan holds up for 3 months, it is likely you can continue. Show your plan to someone who knows business and proceed from that point

Do not spend money on business plan software these tend to be complicated and onerous to complete. The key is to be able to write your idea down on paper to see connections, opportunities and insights and problems you did not uncover.

Each page or slide should be 4-6 bullet points with small tables used to present information simply, such as forecast income and expenditure. By using this method, you can go back and forward through your pages/slides as you develop the plan and idea and insights occur. It really is that simple to start.

My Index is as follows.

1 Idea

2 USP (Unique Selling Proposition)

3 Objectives

4 SWOT (Strengths, Weaknesses, opportunities, Threats)

5 PESTLE (Political, Economic, Social, Technological, Legal, Environmental

Six Marketing

6.1 Product

6.2 People

6.3 Price

6.4 Place

6.5 Promotion

6.6 Positioning

6.7 Package

6.8 Competition

Seven Resources

7.1 Equipment

7.2 People

7.3 Property

Eight Finances

8.1 income

8.2 Expenditure

8.3 Capital

8.4 Profit and Loss / Cash Flow

8.5 Funding

9 Risk

10 Strategy

Appendix A Research

None of these sections should be complicated. The idea is to create a simple outline of your business. Enough to be able to prove to yourself and to others that the idea will work.

Look at any point your business relies on to succeed and ask: 'Have I proved that point?' If not go and prove your idea works or change the plan.

If the plan relies on selling 5000 items a year does the plan prove the numbers of potential buyers who are prepared to buy the item at the price they are sold at?

The Business Plan is the cornerstone of your success in Business. I will explain why your plan is so important. I will explain the sections of the Plan which are Business Context, Marketing, Finances and lastly Governance.

Why do I need a Business Plan?

It is so much better to find your idea does not work on paper before investing money. Your Plan helps you to achieve complete clarity of your concept. A written plan helps you to extract the most from your idea, prompts you to research the data that proves your idea and reveals both new ideas and hidden flaws. The plan may show you why in its initial form the idea will not work or might prompt a better way of doing the business that will work, spectacularly well.

Who Needs Business Plans?

You do. The plan contains your basic assumptions and forecasts. These will set your initial direction and enable you to refer to them if things don't quite work out to understand why and to make corrections. Your family might read the plan if they are to support you or be impacted by the Business, as they surely will. Your advisers will look first at your Plan to understand the idea and what your business is seeking to achieve.

Certainly, anyone who invests or is providing a loan including your Bank Manager will want to scrutinize your Business Plan.

Using my technique, I have drafted over 100 Business Plans for new businesses ideas. Only 10% moved on to full written plans so these examples helped me find 90 ideas that would not work well or not work yet.

I wrote a plan for every business idea that I had, some serious and some less so, designed to investigate an idea further. I have written plans for businesses in action but going wrong. I created plans to clarify new initiatives for growth in existing businesses. A business plan is a flexible tool used in any business circumstance.

This approach is called a proof of concept. Building your concept is the most important work. Prove your business works.

Only once I am satisfied the outline Plan is solid and I have extracted the best insights and ideas, will I commit time to a full written version. This is an efficient way of working useful both for new ideas and ventures already launched new and old.

Use the common Apple Apps like Keynote, Pages and Numbers or Microsoft Office. I predominantly use PowerPoint and Excel for this purpose. I use these more expensive pieces of software to provide me with for client compatibility. Excellent free Google equivalents are great for the start-up enterprise.

1. Concept or Idea

The first slide is Concept in 6 bullet points describe your idea. Chose every word carefully.

This slide becomes your *elevator speech* if someone asked what your business is, you would be able to describe your business in 30 seconds, the time between floors).

2 USP

Your *Unique Selling Proposition* states

What is different about your business?

Why will people come to you and not a competitor or similar business?

What problem does your business solve for your customer?

Why will they keep coming back?

Why will they refer their friends to you?

3 Objectives

A Business without Objectives is like a football match without goal posts. Many businesses start without objectives and hence without direction. You cannot know how your business is performing without something to perform against. Making enough to live on, is not a real Objective. Waiting to see how you get on is a flawed approach. Starting a Business in no way qualifies as an Objective.

A lack of Objectives and vague over-simple Objectives will negatively impact your ability to optimise your Business.

Write down 6-10 objectives. Ensure that they can be measured if they cannot, write out what success would look like if they are achieved. Specify the time by which each Objective will be achieved.

There is a debate as to how difficult to achieve objectives should be. I suggest objectives be tough enough to force you to come up with new ideas to hit them or find ways to be more productive. Making Objectives easy is tempting so that you feel the satisfaction of achieving them and ticking them off. Resist this temptation. Use objectives to pull you towards a better future.

I find that Annual Objectives are best for smaller businesses. Annual Objectives are the norm in bigger businesses although I can make a strong argument for longer periods, to prevent too short term a focus. Split your objectives into quarterly, monthly and weekly targets.

I personally love Objectives and I will find ways to achieve the toughest of these.

Set quarterly milestones to hit to achieve your annual goals from the start. In this way you can set your actions around what needs to be done to achieve an objective. At least I recommend that you take the time to review your progress against Objectives every quarter or every month. Don't write them and ignore them. Use your Objectives to keep you on track and refocus your activity to hit them. If you hit them within the year reset them and strive to achieve more.

On occasions I have set some objectives which describe an improbable but exciting future. This forces me to work out new ways to hit stretch targets.

Have I always achieved them? No, but I tried hard to find a way until timed ran out. Sometimes in trying I achieved considerably more than I ever would think possible and would certainly not have managed if I had set less ambitious objectives. Sometimes I achieved what I or others would describe as impossible. These occasions have been the most rewarding in my life.

What does your impossible success look like? What is stopping you from setting an Objective around that?

4 SWOT

SWOT stands for:

Strengths, Weaknesses, Opportunities and Threats. These are a key part of your Business Plan. These set the context for your business idea. SWOT are framed in the present i.e. the conditions which currently exist.

Strengths: Your Strengths are those things which will propel your business forward. They might include expertise, specific product knowledge or expertise, market contacts, or anything which provide a tail wind for your achieving your business success.

Weaknesses: Are you are aware of things which might impede your success and include competitors, market issue or anything that creates a head wind.

Opportunities: What did you read or learn that might prove a wave you ride or a wind below your sails or anything that might be grasped to improve your chances of success?

Threats: What problems or issues might lie in wait to trap or prevent your business success? These come from anywhere. These include those worst fears lurking in the depths of your brain. The issues you might suspect but chose to ignore for now.

Bounce around from one slide to the other developing your thoughts. Develop a healthy knowledge of yourself. This is invaluable in business

5 PESTLE

This sets the environment with which your business is interacting. The 6 topics map your Business Environment. What is going on in the world your business is going to be operating in? The purpose of this is to check that it is an idea which meets its market, an idea at the right time or to think of new ideas to capitalize on market conditions.

Finally, we want to map out the much wider Business Scenario that you plan to engage with using a technique called a PESTLE to prompt your thinking.

These stand for:

P: Politics

E: Economy

S: Social

T: Technology

L: Legislation

E: Environmental

Against each I list a further 6 -8 bullet points.

As I proceed, I am prompted to add further bullets to my SWOT and to my PESTLE developing a wide scenario of the business environment I plan to engage with.

Politics

In this list how the political environment impacts your business

Swings to the right or the left

Instability cause by policies of particular leaders

Wars or crises

New Policies

Economics

Currency fluctuations

Consumer confidence, spending or saving

Tax changes

Social

Are people starting their own businesses or seeking security in employment?

What trends are emerging in society?

Technology

What technologies are emerging?

How are existing technologies changing?

How is technology in your chosen area moving?

Legal

What impact is law or proposed law having on your business field?

Are Business laws changing generally or in your business sector?

Environmental

What impact is global warming having on your business or might in future?

Are changing weather patterns an issue?

Are environmental trends impacting your business, customers or supplier?

Does improved sustainability give your business an edge?

I briefly outlined a few things that you might be prompted to list. By brainstorming these topics, you create some insights that can help to shape your Strategy, or you highlight risks you need to manage. I put new points into my SWOT after completing a PESTLE as new Opportunities or Threats emerge.

Your view on these trends i.e., agree or disagree does not matter. Notice them and record them in under these headings.

Historic Event Impacts

To better understand your Business Opportunities and Threats you can take the big items and see how these impacted similar businesses historically.

I like to make a list of historic issues which arose in the industry or environment you might be choosing to engage with and the consequences of these historic events. These might include power cuts, strikes, short-term working, wars, pandemics or indeed any event that injured the sector. List each event and its consequences. As you proceed you might add things to your Threats as additional bullet points.

With this mapped out I can develop a strategy that capitalizes on the Opportunities building on my Strengths and mitigates the Threats and Weaknesses. A strategy that is well-equipped to navigate current challenges and the recurrence of any historic ones.

Last time politics swung to the left or right what happened to your type of business, what happens during times of petrol shortages?

Once you compete these slides you see the context your business will launch and develop against. Did completing these give you new thoughts and ideas did you go back to change the SWOT? Did you change your Objectives or refine your Idea?

6 Marketing

This is the most critical part of your plan to start building the developed idea.

Most of your research will be to substantiate your claims that you can produce products or services that sell

That sufficient customers exist to keep selling

The price point you chose makes our business viable

You can reach these customers

You can do it better or differently from the Competition

6.1 Products

What products or services are you selling?

Remember ancillary products

My video business sold graphics, hosting, different versions for web, Facebook etc. in addition to videos.

We did corporate, SME, Private, Documentaries and more

What would your customers buy along with your product?

Are there different levels of your product?

6.2 Place

Where is your market geographically? Is local passing trade your market, are your customers national, international? If so where? Is internet based? English speaking? Is China an option?

6.3 People

Who is your customer can you describe her? You may be able to describe a few different customers.

In your market local, regional, national, global how many of them exist are they people or businesses, clubs, charities, government bodies?

How many could you bring your product to?

Are your customers other businesses?

Break these down by sex, age, other categories e.g. home-owners, renters. The better you can refine their characteristics the better they can be targeted especially with online advertising.

Every category refines your marketing approach

6.4 Price

How much will you sell your product/service for?

What is its cost of production?

Are you trying to price high or cheaply compared to the market?

Why is that the right pricing policy?

What prices do you require achieve to break-even?

What are similar or substitute products priced at?

6.5 Position

Where are you positioning your product or service in the market?

Is your product a more expensive luxury item with high service levels and a high degree of customization?

Is your approach minimal cost, mass market cheap and cheerful?

6.6 Package

What add-ons are you offering to distinguish your product or services from others?

When I employ tradesmen, I want to know that they have insurance for example.

6.7 Promotion

Can you reach enough people to make your business work?

How will you do this? Prove this.

What will your avenues of promotion be?

How many potential customers might you contact to make a sale? Is this a reasonable estimate?

Face to face with your customer group offers the best conversion rate.

For a high-volume sales business example, for conversion rates I very roughly use 1:6, face-to-face, phone calls might be 1:12. A written approach is nearer 1:50 or worse.

What is the ratio of cost of marketing to profits made? Does the cost of marketing justify the returns?

6.8 Digital

I now create a separate slide to cover how to capitalize on the digital world

Millions of websites are live, how is yours found? The quality of your site plays a part in ranking along with media content and the frequency of updates. Which Social Media channels are you on? How do customers find you?

You can buy prime search positions at a cost. SEO, search engine optimization, is not as useful as it used to be. Google, Facebook, Twitter and LinkedIn Ads should be considered but these differ in effectiveness by business type. I recommend getting expert advice before spending your cash.

Can you invest in a professional website designer / marketing strategist or will you use free or low-cost options? Your decision depends on what you expect from your site.

Social Media

Advertising via Social Media is a huge fast evolving specialist topic but as important to smaller businesses as to multi-nationals This is an area to employ expert advice.

Twitter is a signpost only, but free and numerous people form entrepreneurial groups who might become customers. Check their follower numbers to see how genuine these are.

Use social media, a blog or Facebook page to create a community of fans.

6.9 Competition

Is someone already doing what your idea is?

How is your idea differentiated?

What things can be substituted for your product or services they are also competitors.

What types of competition do you face?

Where are they located? Same street? Examine their products, people, place, price and promotion

What will make them worry about you?

Can your idea be copied? Can your idea be protected?

Did your projections allow for competitors winning sales over you?

7. Resources

The section on resources provides a view on the people you might employ the premises you require plus the equipment needed to make store and sell your products or services. At the planning stage challenge every penny of your proposed spend.

7.1 Equipment

Whether it is large scale machinery or tools, or office equipment most business types will have some requirements here. This is an area to be careful not to generate a shopping list of nice things to have. Identify the minimum equipment essential for your business.

7.2 People

Will you employ staff? Can you use sub-contractors, or will it just be yourself in your business?

7.3 Property

Property is a big issue. Whether you purchase or rent it becomes a long-term fixed cost. When times are tough property is difficult to get away from. Property comes with associated costs including insurance, maintenance, rates and outfitting. Its type and location are critical decisions.

Your property becomes a part of your brand and promotion. Do you want passing trade or logistics convenience? What part of your business does your property play? Property is a decision on its own but completely intwined with other aspects of your plan.

Section 8 Finances

For the non-accountant, this section of your plan can be difficult. At this outline stage I favor a simple approach to provide a framework around which to build a good plan. More detail can be added at a later stage with professional help if appropriate.

8.1 Income

Income is estimated at by arriving at the number of sales you will make in your different products and services, less the cost of these sales.

If I make widgets. My Selling price is £5 but it costs £2.50 to make each one or if I buy it manufactured this is called buying price. If I sell 400 widgets a week, my turnover, (money generated) is £2000 but my income is £1000.

I use a simple table a row for each product and service. Column one is product, column two is number of sales, column three is cost of production (or buying price), column four is selling price, column five is profit per item, column six is total profit for that item.

For my widget example this would look like:

Income

Product	Sales	BP	SP	Profit	Total
Widget A	400	2.50	5.00	2.5	900

I also create a second income table showing the income spread across months. This would show the build up from launch and seasonal variances.

Jan	Feb	Mar	Apr	May	Jun	Jul	Aug	Sep	Oct	Nov	Dec
0	600	1200	1800	2000	2400	3000	3600	3600	4000	5000	3000

It would be unreasonable to assume that I would sell 900 every week from launch so I account for these differences.

For these simplified tables I have assumed a business launch in January.

8.2 Expenditure

For this section I again use a simple table listing the overheads my business has. This will include salary, property costs, vehicle costs, insurance, professional fees, licenses and permits, office costs. Marketing costs. This can be a long list or a simple list. You are trying to arrive at a good estimate of the cost of running your business. I usually, do this by creating a month-by-month table as some payments are monthly, others quarterly others yearly. Some payments are in advance others in arrears. Using a monthly chart is useful for the cash flow table.

Expenditure

	Month	Quarter	Total
Wages	900		10800
Vehicle costs	200		2400
Property costs	500	200	6800
Marketing		500	2000
Total			22000

This table shows the expenditure month by month

Jan	Feb	Mar	Apr	May	Jun	Jul	Aug	Sep	Oct	Nov	Dec
1600	1600	2300	1600	1600	2300	1600	1600	2300	1600	1600	2300

8.3 Profit and Loss / Cash Flow

The profit and loss account is another simple table. I create a table with a column for each month. The first row is income, the second-row expenditure, the third-row is the cash flow. Remember it might take some time to generate the income you hope for as your customers become aware of your products or services. Your expenditure is relentless. Use the figures from your income and expenditure tables.

Cash Flow

By taking the monthly Income and Expenditure figures calculating the is a matter of subtracting the expenditure from the income and adding the monthly balance to the previous months total to create a running balance figure.

	Jan	Feb	Mar	Apr	May	Jun	Jul	Aug	Sep	Oct	Nov	Dec
Inc	0	600	1200	1800	2000	2400	3000	3600	3600	4000	5000	3000
Exp	1600	1600	2300	1600	1600	2300	1600	1600	2300	1600	1600	2300
Cash	-1600	-2600	-3700	-3500	-3100	-3000	-1600	400	1500	3900	7200	7900

8.4 Capital

Identify the money required to start your business and run it. You also need money to meet your outgoings until the business makes a profit is your capital. Items to be bought, deposits and advance payments all get included in capital.

There are costs which need to be met from day one in your business when no income is being made. These include wages, rent stock purchase costs among a number of other important payments. You might be given credit by suppliers. The next section your cash flow will show the money that you are short and need to have the capital from the start to fund.

In the Cash Flow table, I have used my Income number to estimate my monthly income build up. My expenditure is spread over a flat £1600 a month outgoing plus quarterly payments to illustrate how cash flow is inconsistent and usually negative for the period of launching a business. At one point in the above example your business is short of £3500. You either need to have that as a capital reserve or have your bank allow an overdraft facility to help you over this period. Notice as well that in this example the business is in negative cash flow every month from January to July only narrowly becoming positive in August.

This is a highly simplified example but hopefully illustrates the points I am making. You might well take over a year before cash flow is positive. Some business never get past this stage without substantial working capital provisions.

8.5 Funding

Having identified your capital requirements a slide identifying where this money will be sourced is worth including. I mention funding in a Pitfall 59. You might source your capital from your own savings, by borrowing from family and friends. A good business plan might secure funding from a bank or from angel investors. A new innovative idea might be able to generate capital through crowdfunding. In businesses like pubs suppliers can provide money in exchange for a commitment to use their product.

9 Risks

Create a Table 4 columns several rows - The columns are headed: Risk, Probability, Impact, Mitigation. Every row lists a separate risk.

Brainstorm all possible risks and write these in column-one. In column-two assess the likelihood of this risk occurring, I use high, medium and low as the options. Column-three shows the impact of that risk on your business, again use high, medium or low, in the list column, column-four, write the steps you can take to prevent, pre-empt or to minimise the impact of this risk.

I reorder the risks so that risks which have high probability and high impact are at the top, low probability, low impact at the bottom.

Let me illustrate the importance of this section with a story of a close friend of mine. He ran a successful food product business. The business was growing, and they won many awards. When the UK voted to leave the EU overnight the pound fell 30% increasing his Euro based costs as most of his raw ingredients came from the EU.

He was furious and on Social Media decried the stupidity of leave voters and generally vented his anger and frustration.

As a businessperson his view on whether the UK left or remained was irrelevant. His task was to identify and assess the risk of either outcome to his business. Then deal appropriately with that in advance.

To create a risk matrix takes no more than an hour. His risks were currency fluctuations, import restrictions and supply and customer access. These would all shown up as major risks to his business. Having identified the possible risks and the impact on his business the process would be to brainstorm ideas to mitigate the risks.

In this example he might identify possible UK suppliers and created options with them. He might put some money into Euros when the rate was favorable and kept these for times when the exchange rates swung against him.

Many in the same circumstances moan about their EU customers being more difficult to trade with in the future. They ought to find customers in other markets and diversify their exposure. Business is about problem solving irrespective of politics.

The significant issue to grasp is that to separate your own strongly held views and instead work with probability and mitigation. Brexit was at best a 50:50 probability so all businesses ought to identify the risks and indeed the opportunities in either outcome for the business to thrive. You want to be the one that can say.

"This was a great result for our business" irrespective of what the result might be!

Section 10 Strategy

Write the critical factors you will take to achieve your business Objectives.

Extract these from the slides you created

I often put a slide headed insight after each section

Strategy includes what you won't do, won't sell, won't sell to. This can be as significant to your success as what you will do, you simply cannot resource doing everything.

Your focus here ought to be around Products, Pricing, Place, People and promotion. What are the options to achieve your Objectives?

What is the route map you are creating for business success? This may include all aspects of your plan. Starting in the evenings and weekends while still working your job, using your house as your office. Your marketing ideas will be significant inputs to your strategy but think broadly and creatively about all aspects.

Appendix A Research

One thing I learnt as a Management Consultant was the value of getting really great at research. The young consultants that worked for me were able to find anything I asked for on the internet. Ask yourself the question; 'What should I be able to demonstrate with data for someone to believe my business plan'?

I found:

the number of people of a specific age group within a certain mileage radius of a proposed restaurant to demonstrate the potential client base.

the number of businesses and clubs in a country to assess the potential sales for a video advertising company.

the growth and death rate of new businesses in the UK Before writing this book. These are supplied in annual government statistics.

Only use official statistics if possible. The internet is full of wrong information used to justify particular points of view or to sell newspapers and magazines or to create a stir. Check that your research is valid. Most of what you need is contained in official government reports.

Become good at finding information by learning how to use Google or your favourite search engine. The search engines all provide free guides in how to make the best use of their site.

I generate lots of research supporting my plan

I use this section to reference where the research sits. e.g., I copy and paste from the web especially metric type information, so that I have the information on a Word or Pages or Google docs document.

Go Back and iterate you plan

Make changes to refine and improve the plan.

Pay attention to the *insights, connections and relationships* you gleaned in the exercise. I insert slides headed insights and ideas at the end of sections to record these as I go.

Watch or read something associated with your business to create more ideas.

Do some early actions that would improve your knowledge and plan

Keep revisiting everything for 4-6 weeks

If your plan is holding up, ask a trusted positive friend with some expertise to look at the plan. Do not ask Joe in the pub.

Now write your plan as a full document again the idea will develop and grow

If your plan is not holding up to scrutiny celebrate you saved a lot of time and money and heartache.

Could you change something about your plan to invent a different approach that would succeed?

Put the plan aside where you can come back to review in the future

This now becomes a part of your learning.

Brainstorm another idea don't be put off, as I said I shelved 90% of my business plans. Some might have worked and in some circumstances, I might be prepared to take the risk.

I often realize that the business idea has not generated the excitement, energy and passion to have me pursue further.

Celebrate ideas that you prove do not work. You have saved time, money and energy.

In many cases you need to spend time doing a business the wrong way to find the right way to succeed. Things change, you change, markets change, competitors fall out of the market.

A client of mine had 4-6 false starts in business, these cost a lot of money, stress, time and some friendships, but he found a way through. His first idea was a complete non-starter. He moved using his learning to a new version that worked, and he was soon pulling together knowledge and a saleable skill set and the habits he needed to succeed. Every idea that failed had provide the learning, endurance, contacts and energy to make his final business a great success.

He took learning and contacts from the failures to make the final business successful.

This is a hard, but he was young and had many lessons to learn. At the end he survived and was a better businessman. My advice is to do as much on paper as you can, its less costly, less stressful and you can be more objective about what success requires in your chosen field.

Pitfall 14 A Failure to Grasp the Big Picture

The failure to grasp the *big picture* is a failing in many new businesspeople. I am referring to a failure to grasp the fundamentals of the business as it relates to the business environment and current trends.

New entrepreneurs, with so much to do, are often afraid to identify and pursue what is really important and what makes the business perform.

I once worked for a diving company owned by a wealthy individual, Walter Wolf. His ownership style was light touch. He phoned once a week to ask a single question.

How many divers are working this week?' He understood that the people, processes and systems in place would ensure everything would go well but key to the business success was the number of divers which represented the amount of work won, income and profit. He did not need more. A lesson in watching the big picture.

What single question might let you know that your business was succeeding?

Would you like to succeed bigger and faster? A key ingredient of the most successful entrepreneurs is their ability to see and understand the big picture. Be able to rise over the small stuff, the minutia, emotion and fuzzy thinking to get to the essence of any issue. Then you can see what really matters.

When I worked for Shell a part of your annual appraisal was a score for what they termed 'Helicopter Vision'. The ability to rise above the daily dramas and take an overview of the bigger picture.

This is the ability to separate the Important from the Urgent. Too often we react to the ringing telephone or the shouting client. This is urgent not necessarily important. Some urgent things are important if that bell is a fire alarm for example, that is urgent and important to react to. We need to separate important things which may be urgent but not critical from those that are most important and prioritize these.

New or inexperienced businesspeople tend to confuse urgency with importance. Be clear about the distinction and prioritize early. Important things delayed do have a tendency to become both urgent and important.

Prioritize firstly; important and urgent, then important not urgent.

Is anything urgent but not important. Probably not. What are the consequences of not doing it? Is it urgent or is that an illusion you created for yourself?

I remember a client of a friend, a baker whose was struggling with exhaustion and starting to dislike the work he had previously loved. He delivered bread to his customers at 5am every day. The reason was that he did this because his father always did this. His father made bread and delivered the bread at 5am during the war in Germany if he did not deliver the bread, people starved. By the early 21st century in North America no one starves from a late bread delivery. When my friend's client asked his customers if he delivered by 9am would that be an issue. They were happy to receive their daily bread at 9am. He had created a work system which made the wrong things urgent.

Your categorization of urgent and important can be deeply rooted in your thinking which is hard to retrain yourself around.

Anything you rank as urgent but not important needs reappraising and a specific time or date set for when that should be done.

Finally, ignore anything neither important nor urgent.

Most successful people keep daily to do lists. I keep 3 separate lists:

One: priority: Do today (which I restricted to a few items)

Two: do at some point: When the today list is clear, and you have time to spare.

Three: Don't do. Write the action down as an action you won't do now but will retain for the future. In this way I don't clutter my life with dozens of insignificant actions, nor fill my memory with things I need to remember at some unspecified future point. In this way I don't forget things that might be useful in the future.

A further tip is to maintain somewhere, a full 12 months of future actions. In this way you can put schedule actions in the weeks or months when they ought to be done.

Seeing the big picture is about being productive. Train yourself to stop yourself doing things that are not important and work out exactly what is productive.

As an example, take my proposed podcast series. Productive is writing, recording, editing; publishing episodes and promoting the episode on social media; community building by answering questions and interacting with my audience.

Unproductive Is researching new types of recording equipment to buy; developing future series and most other things.

Start to train yourself by trying this technique.

Plan your day, first thing in the morning, look at your list does each task take you closer to your objectives? Is there something else which would? Eliminate anything not productive.

Do the most productive important thing first. This is often the activity that you least like doing. Do it!

Are you avoiding difficult things in favour of easy things you enjoy doing or can tick off as completed? Often the difficult things are the important things that bring you closer to your objectives.

Follow this routine for the whole week and you will make progress and as you follow this approach you will find fewer urgent things arising in your day. Why? Because you did them because they were important and, did them in plenty of time. Kept your accounts, submitted tax returns, you found time for these and got them done.

Procrastination more than anything is the thief of your time and your success. Procrastination drives you towards not urgent and not important activity. Ensure a warning in your brain goes off when you waste time in procrastination activities. Stop and go and do the next productive thing.

Pitfall 15 A Failure to Introduce Scalability

Imagine, things are going well, your business is working, you are making money. The issue is like many small businesses you are not making enough money. You are only narrowly breaking even; you kept your own salary at a minimum and are struggling to find ways to make more. Often the pitfall is, that your business lacks sufficient scale; insufficient resources; insufficient customers; insufficient income.

If your aim is to grow a substantial business, then scalability is vital to how you grow. Scalability means that if your idea works and generates reliable profits you would be able to replicate that model with additional products in a different area or country. Franchise businesses work in this way. Too many businesses are so focussed on a tiny slice of the market and start with good results, but these fall off leaving the owner nowhere to turn. You can't extract more business from existing clients, and they resist price rises.

A failure to increase prices can also be an issue. When costs increase or you see that you are offering more value than you are charging you sometimes require to increase your charges. You can start with new customers moving into existing customers. You might lose some or you might not. The trick is to be confident that you offer value for money. Some small customers you can't afford to carry.

Businesses are either growing or shrinking. To sit at a steady state turning over the same amount year by year is rare. For no other reason this is because your sales start to saturate your own market. If you are installing conservatories for example, every conservatory installed is one less potential customer in the future. If you are designing web sites every website designed takes that company out of the market for a website for a few years, but they may need other services.

You could market websites to a broader community or using the same infrastructure offer a wider range of products which build on the initial website sale if your business was scalable.

No magic bullets solve this challenge. Clear thinking is the answer. Take the time to think this through to achieve the benefits of scale in your business.

In a recent business I was investigating. The owner had a great insight. He realized that he was the limitation on growth. He did all the work and did not trust others to deliver as well. As the business grew, he only had so many hours in the day.

The solution was for him to manage the business and train and coach others to deliver. In this way, his income became increased by as many clients that he attracted and as many staff as were sourced and trained to the required quality level.

Get yourself out of the way and let your business expand!

Pitfall 16 Poor Strategy

To discuss issues around poor Strategy. I will describe what Strategy is. I did provide some ideas in the Fundamentals Section of this Topic. Unfortunately, business writers can be divided on this topic. Here is my view.

Strategy is a changing and evolving high-level plan, like a battlefield general, you as the owner of the strategy are assembling and directing your troops (resources) to achieve various objectives. You decide who attacks what, where and when as the battle changes.

Attacks succeed or fail; your opponent make different moves some of which play into your strategy whilst others thwart your intentions. Your troops are the resources of your business: staff, equipment, money, your own time.

The key features of strategy are:

Over time as the situation changes the strategy is altered.

The strategy is based on an understanding of the circumstances you face at any time

The strategy interprets what is happening before you

You have many options, but these can be mutually exclusive. You make one choice with your available resources, so you don't have the resources to simultaneously chose another option.

This means what you chose not to do is as important as choosing what to do.

Every choice has its time, so strategy is made along a timeline of moving pieces.

Strategy has winners and losers.

The foundation for your strategy comes from the scenario you face in your business at launch. We create this scenario by reference to our SWOT and PESTLE the playing field upon which your Strategy will play out.

We then establish further our pieces in play. Product or Services are the players we are betting our success on.

People are your potential Clients; we hope they will purchase our products at the prices we pitch them at. Our research ought to have satisfied us that the markets we target, in the way we chose, has sufficient numbers of clients to support out enterprise.

Price is also researched and it is pitched to attract enough customers at a profitable rate to move things on.

Place is the location we think best for our business to operate. The geography of our chosen battlefield. We capitalise on the layout of the land we see in front of us. Price is the calibre of our weapons.

Promotion is the way we chose to target our customers, bringing them into our sights before we secure their business.

Many other variables oblige us to make decisions on in our strategy.

A useful feature of strategy is called 'enablers'. Enablers are things that give us an advantage over others. An enabler might be a product, a key skill or sometimes a process. Take a drain cleaning business. The local norm may be to clean drains with push rods. The business calculates that they can profitably clean more drains using a pressure cleaning system. This is an Enabler.

I recall once a company in a group of similar companies was achieving much better attendance records than the others. They revealed, on questioning, that everyone off ill had a personal interview with a manager on the day of their return to see how they were and if any changes to working arrangements were needed to accommodate them. Irrespective of the reasons why, this was a huge enabler for their productivity.

The Strategy you formulate decides what emphasis to put on the components of your business, given your interpretation of the prevailing business conditions and tends.

Your Product mix can be varied. You can choose which markets to operate in and which to ignore. You can alter your pricing strategy, use different advertising and marketing and apply your resources in a different way.

As your business develops you will look at historic events and trends to better understand and predict the future ones your strategy addresses. History has a bad habit of repeating itself.

I tend to keep my Strategy to about 10 key points. Simple to understand, simple to share and simple enough to guide your actions. This will rule how I attack the market for the next period.

I measure the outcomes to see if my strategy needs varying. I once remember discussing which clients to target in a strategy discussion. We picked on one particular company (Shell), we had no business with at that point. We identified which contacts we knew. Within a year we had achieved 4 high-paying pieces of work. I guarantee without writing this in our Strategy we would not have had this success.

In highly competitive markets monitor your competitors. Your competitors may offer products or services which directly compete with your own. Monitor competition from different product which achieve the same outcome, so called substitutes.

For example: A piano company only competed with other piano manufacturers until the advent of digital pianos which emerged as a substitute. Next, electronic boxes (synth modules) were produced that were played with control keyboards which then in turn were supplanted by software instruments.

You can see how the conditions of this market moved and how competition moved in parallel. Those whose strategy did not change or identify the shift were left with a smaller albeit niche market.

A strategy should be robust enough to last for a year. Should there be a big change you need to be flexible and prepared to reframe it. The 2020 pandemic is one such example. Few strategies survived this event. For long term decisions a five-year strategy is also worth having. This will address the more permanent decisions such as property, products and equipment where rapid changes are difficult or costly.   Your one-year strategy will mainly cover staff, clients and marketing.

Pitfall 17 Inability to Create a Money Machine

Many new businesses fail because they don't have a repeatable formula. If every job or sales is a one off, the time taken will lead to failure. My IT client produced web sites for a living but at £2000 each the costs were more than new businesses afforded which resulted in too few customers to sustain the business. He tried several approaches, higher costs, larger clients. He eventually designed a money-making machine.

He did the same quality website by replicating the more expensive ones which clients had failed to pay for. He developed and used actions. An action completes numerous programming steps at the push of a key. This produced high quality web sites with less programming time. He then charged a monthly fee for the site and its hosting. New businesses could afford this as their businesses grew where a one-off lump sum was too expensive for them.

This model was to find a customer, initiate the actions, set up payment, turn the handle print more money. A money-machine. He used that model for a while and created a more lucrative money machine.

Your money machine may be simple, or complex, but should be reliable and repeated. Generating work, revenue and profits.

The move from expensive owned software to monthly subscriptions is a further example. Major software providers found that either their clients bought once and avoided buying again or potential clients bought pirate software copies, scared away by high prices. They got around this by providing monthly subscriptions. They charged smaller monthly amounts and clients received updates whenever they were complete rather than with annual releases. The smaller fees encouraged people to sign up. The constant free upgrade releases encouraged loyalty and greatly reduced the use of pirate software. In the end revenues increased and this created a reliable money machine.

Key Features of a money machine are:

A repeatable model

Meeting a need in the way that clients most require

Continuous demand

No 'yea buts' in other words sold on a *take it or leave it* basis for customers that don't fit the model

Simple to sell, simple to implement.

Readily resourced, if demand were to rapidly increase the resources of sufficient skill levels quickly assembled.

Not replicable, to minimize competition. In my client's case this was achieved by the way in which the actions were designed, loading and customising the sites, installing security and e-commerce if required which gave more revenue opportunities

This delivers a sustainable product with add on business opportunities for future customization and ancillary services. Every year over 300,000 new businesses are created which ensured a steady supply of potential new customers.

Pitfall 18 A Lack of Ambition

I advise new businesses to err on the side of caution in their Business plans.

Following the crowd and keeping to conventional approaches might constrict your business in its early stages when you need to enjoy some growth and success to keep the cash flowing and attract customers.

A failure to aim high might mean opportunities are lost. Over prudence can leave a new business at the mercy of established players who have the financial strength to undercut and take a more approach by utilizing superior resources.

You might want to aim much higher by preparing a more expansive version of your plan to test for more dramatic possibilities. A failure to test this might lead to ignoring the true potential. Be prepared and have thought out this possibility.

Be bold and brave as a trial. Consider what you might do to be much more successful, before landing on your initial Objectives. Stretch targets give you the freedom to open your mind and without the restrictions of 'current thinking' to invent, innovate and uncover new ways of doing things.

Be prudent in financial matters but bold in Operations. Generate some momentum in your business by getting your name about and delivering quality work and superior service.

Investigate every avenue for delivering a better product. Clear thinking is your most valuable business asset. As suggested, do a lot of your thinking on paper and some on the wall. Graphic boards and flip charts are great for mapping out new ideas. This can be useful for seeing relationships, links and key insights many people work best graphically. By getting ideas on paper in writing or drawings, revisit them as new ideas emerge, adding them into your records.

Once ideas are on paper it is great how your brain develops them when you are not consciously thinking about them, and sometimes when you are asleep. Ideas often come in the shower first thing in the morning. I don't know why or how, but they do. First job every morning is to write down these ideas or solutions to problems your subconscious mind has solved. If this works for your you will have a powerful business tool at your disposal.

This approach might produce different plans. One for a conservative approach and the other a more aggressive viral version. Whatever you might be able to modify your plan to benefit from the best of both in your final approach.

Pitfall 19 Taking the Wrong Advice

New entrepreneurs ought to look for advice. This advice comes with a warning. Advice is cheap these days and everyone is an 'expert' or, so they think.

If you are fortunate you will have a good network, building a network is an important life skill, for the entrepreneur.

Many successful women and men are willing to help new entrepreneurs when asked. Be patient and not wasteful of their time.

Too many entrepreneurs ask family or friends, colleagues or fellow drinkers. They are invariably well-meaning and feel their duty is to protect you from yourself. They know nothing useful and give advice based on their worst fears or jealousies.

Advice is most useful from people who have done what you want to do or are professional in the area you want advice about. Who would you ideally want to advise you in your new business? Maybe no one in your network but someone might know someone else. If not, your local business start-up organisation will be able to help.

Again, be wary. Government organizations all too often attract well-meaning amateurs or failed professionals whose knowledge and methods may be outdated. You might be better seeking advice from someone who is successful in the business if your area of business needs real expertise. Make a phone call asking for 5 minutes of their time. Go prepared with the few key questions you hope they might be prepared to answer. They might refuse, nothing lost, phone someone else.

If you have a brief business plan take the opportunity to show the plan to an adviser, your bank, accountant and lawyer. Do not show the plan to everyone you know. Show it to those who are successful in a different field or have expertise within a specific business area but be prepared for some negative comments. Be prepared to investigate their observations further if they throw up useful if unwelcome insights.

Do not use this process as a marketing exercise. You might get some breaks from it and research of customers is frequently a marketing exercise. Think of these phone calls, you might have received, that start:

'I am not selling anything. I wanted to ask you a few questions.'

They are selling something. Try to separate your research and advice from sales or your advisers will stop you in your tracks.

If you need to research potential clients, ask simple open questions about what they think about the type of service or product you are offering. You will recognise that your customers and advisers are the source of two different types of information.

Pitfall 20 Failure to Manage the Downside

Society suggests currently that to achieve we ought to be positive, optimistic and aim high. This is true, but its converse is not true.

Our negative thoughts, worries and fears are useful and inform our route to success as much as the positivity by telling us the things to avoid or put actions in place to mitigate against.

By surfacing and addressing the potential pitfalls, we set our business up for success. In the first stages of our excitement and eagerness to proceed and do well, voices of doom and despair will be common. Stories of those who tried, failed and fell. Shooting down those who try to step out from the pack is unfortunately common but should inspire you to show them they are wrong.

Whilst tempted to ignore these and minimize their views, consider them without emotion or defensiveness. They might unknowingly be giving you the route to success. An example of this was a book I was writing for a market which was a busy group of people.

My wife said, these people don't have time to read. That will not succeed. I had not really considered this in my planning. I stopped stood back and thought further what if I made sure than my book included an audio version to be listened to as this group worked. This was a good idea which I missed by being too defensive.

Break-Even Point (BEP)

A key tool in your business planning is to calculate your break-even point. The break-even point is the number and value of sales or services delivered required to meet business expenditure. Above the BEP you make profits, below you make losses. Understanding this point lets you assess whether your business plan through the years can consistently and realistically exceed this point.

BEP is exceptionally useful because, it is easy in the excitement of launching a new venture to base your planning on overoptimistic sales forecasts. By looking at what it takes to break-even and demonstrating through research exactly why this can be achieved, you improve confidence and certainty in your plan. Of course, you might also reveal that a rethink is needed.

You plan demonstrates that you can exceed the BEP all the time because you always need some slack to cover cash flow issues and other setbacks, a break-even business will eventually fail. You need a comfortable margin above the BEP to be profitable, as they say. Not making, losses!

Periodic brainstorming of the Business Risks and review of the mitigation, including insurance is a requirement, at least annually or more if you are facing fast moving change, is imperative.

Pitfall 21 The Paralysis of Analysis

Some people love to analyse business ideas. They are, understandably, nervous of putting aside the security of a job and would train or analyse to the point at which actually starting a business is avoided and never comes.

There is a fine line between over preparation and under preparation before launching a business. This is best described in an example.

Let's say you want to start a market stall selling tourist items. You know the cost for the stall in a location heavily populated by tourists. You have £2000 for stocking your stall.

You could spend time trying to learn what the tourists want to buy, examining different locations, different types of paper bag etc. etc. It is a simple business and does not require much of a Business Plan, although a short one would be helpful.

Alternatively, knowing what you already know, you might visit the local wholesaler and buy £1000 of products. Put them on your stall and see what sells and perfect your selling techniques. Once you have sold enough products go back to the wholesaler and buy more of what sells and similar items and return to your stall and keep selling.

In this second model, you are:

Making money

Improving your skills

Learning exactly what sells

Creating a supplier relationship

Learning about your market

In this example you are building your business plan as you sell. You are getting more detailed information than you can gather online. For this type of business learn as you sell is the right approach. You are running an experiment to prove your business.

This is not infallible nor getting everything out of your idea. You might still need to plan:

How you source your products at better prices?

What next?

What happens outwith the tourist season?

What if you take ill?

How could you expand your business?

Might you operate several stalls?

Do better locations exist?

You have gained useful insights and knowledge as you have worked to answer these questions. Be sure to take the time to stop and think. Effectively this has been a £1000 test of your idea.

Many of my early ventures were of this type. Successful businessmen started on this type of approach; Lord Alan Sugar is one who has stated he adopted this approach.

Try this type of business at least once. You have to buy, sell and deal with the public. You have to stock, shift slow selling lines, barter and face a multitude of business challenges. You will learn a great deal in the process.

Pitfall 22 A Hobby not a Business

Your job or your hobby is an obvious place to begin a business. This depends on, your expertise and motivation. Many businesses start from hobbies that their owners are passionate about. I remember a war gaming business which started in a nearby city. The business sold war gaming sets, pieces and books. Every time I walked past people were in the shop gathered around a table playing war games.

The owner had access to wholesale war game equipment, spent his time war gaming but went bankrupt soon afterwards. Owning a city centre shop had high overheads. Too few customers bought goods to support his business. Those in the shop, including the owner were playing or watching and were not actually spending their money. In truth his business was an extension of his hobby. If he had done any business planning, he would have seen that no real business was possible on this way of working.

This was sad. I am sure that the failure hit him hard. I don't know whether he war-gamed again.

I am not suggesting that hobbies make poor businesses, many are successes. The issue is that making a business from a hobby depends on what you can sell or what service you can provide and how many people will buy.

Far too many hobby businesses, generate hobby income. If your

ambition is to make enough to generate a small income from an extension of your hobby that is fine, as long as you are aware of this.

Beware of changing trends. I do remember a skateboard business started by a passionate young skateboarder. Skateboarding started as a trend but declined, enough to harm his business. Fortunately, he spotted this in time and expanded into ski-ing and snowboarding equipment. This kept him solvent but between the decline in income and the need for more capital to restock, he had two or three lean years and subsequently closed down.

I heard an interesting story recently on the radio. Two young maths graduates enjoyed pole dancing as a sport and hobby but were frustrated that the clothing available in the UK was of poor quality. They started their own business, importing quality clothing from the US and elsewhere. Their business has grown fast, they are now working the business full-time having started in a spare bedroom they now have a warehouse unit, have employed staff and are looking for designers and manufacturers to make their own clothing. A real success story from a hobby.

That was the key. They spotted a problem that needed solving. That problem resonated with their customer base. The business was not designed to let them do more of their hobby but rather to increase the enjoyment of that hobby for others.

One caution. The most successful businesses grown from hobbies end up dramatically reducing both the time and enthusiasm available to undertake your hobby itself. Not a bad thing in the short term.

Your Work is your Hobby

The opposite is also a Pitfall I have observed. When your work becomes your obsession and your hobby. This may seem to be a good thing but if your job becomes your hobby there are factors to be aware of.

I had a cabinet maker do work for me. Wood was his passion every piece was over worked and over engineered. His craftsmanship was exceptional. He would lose track of time when in his workshop he became so engrossed in his work. This led to missed deadlines and embarrassment on his part and frustration on mine.

The solution is never to lose track of the overarching need for the work to be the core the business. The business when successful permits you to live from work you truly enjoy.

Pitfall 23 A Failure to Fully Utilize Assets

A rigid idea of what assets a business requires can result in having too much capital tied up in assets which don't pay their way. Every penny spent on your business has to earn income for you. It is easy to think you need a shop, workshop, vehicle, expensive equipment and so on because that is the norm but fail to consider how every item pays its way.

I know most new businessmen and women are used to sweating or ladies, glowing. Hard work and precarious problems abound in small and medium-sized business. What I am taking about here is making your assets work for you. Make your assets sweat buckets!

I remember speaking to a friend who was about to open a bar and nightclub in an old bank building he had purchased. He was describing the huge overhead he was taking on.

These included the mortgage on the building, rates, insurance and other fixed costs. He owned several nightclubs and that was his business model on this occasion he was adding a bar as well.

I pointed out to him that as his opening hours were 6pm to 3am he was effectively paying for his new building overhead for 24 hours but only earning from the overhead for 9 hours.

I suggested he open for coffee and breakfast in the morning, lunch and afternoon tea. In this way he would earn money for 18 hours a day for the same overhead cost. Of course, he needed a few more staff, utilities and products but when he did the numbers, he revised his design and his plans. Thus, the 'Cafe Bar' was invented. He went on to own several such establishments in his Aberdeen and in London because the model worked.

The most basic model many apply is to work from home using home as accommodation and office space. Home has a lounge with room for a desk and meetings, a toilet and a coffee facility and canteen - the kitchen. If you were creative, could you reduce, cut or share your costs.

List your Assets, premises, vehicles etc. The neighbours upstairs or shop next door might like to share your internet costs. Do you use your van continuously each day or van share with other businesses which need the van at different times? Could your IT manager service all businesses in your street?

Take the example of a chocolate shop, could hours or services be extended? Here are 8 ideas:

Sell online

Give chocolate making classes

Have a table and chairs and in the morning sell hot chocolate and croissants

Offer small groups champagne and chocolate tasting evenings

Offer a wrapped chocolate gift home delivery service

Have a section for chocolate products from other countries

Sell chocolate making supplies

Run chocolate making evening classes

Offer children's parties on quiet afternoons and weekends

To implement any of these ideas means there are problems to be overcome: licences, costs, staffing, new skills. This is what being an entrepreneur involves. I find this the exciting part. I am tempted to purchase a chocolate shop just to try these out!

Every pound or dollar that reduces your overheads or every additional dollar earned without increasing your overheads is added directly to profits or reduces losses. These ideas also add to your income. If you are the business owner you will be used to working more hours than the norm, make your Assets do the same.

A Client's Business has customers world-wide. She uses the fact that the world is open 24 hours a day to service her clients at different times. Her business is expanding, and she will have her office open for 24 hours with 3 shifts of 8 hours. One set of overheads will run 3 times the work. The office, computers, servers, phone system all the assets will benefit from three times the use.

The clock of overheads clicks away incessantly 24 hours a day; rent, running costs, online subscriptions, vehicle tax you pay for 24 hours which do you only use a fraction of the available time. If you run your business 5 days a week 9 - 5pm you are earning income over 40 hours, but a week has 168 hours. You earn from less than 25% of the available resources. 8736 hours in a year are available why use only a fraction of them?

I am not suggesting you can exist without sleep or rest or holidays or indeed run some modern slave trading system, Be creative.

The key insight I think are:

Do not be trapped by a traditional thinking model.

Use your overheads as much as possible? Make them work hard to earn you income

Use 24 hours to maximize income earning opportunities

Be imaginative and creative about sharing the cost of overheads with others.

If you think hard enough about them opportunities always exist.

The biggest trick is to find ways of making income while you are asleep.

Most importantly don't use your business as an excuse for buying 'toys'. I spoke to a young entrepreneur recently who had budgeted for a Drone as he thought this would enhance his website. He confessed he might use this for his business no more than 3 times a year. I suggested he hire or employ a videographer with a drone. If the drone purchase would not pay for itself, buying one was not a good idea. A simple cost benefit analysis would eliminate this.

A bit of imagination and problem solving will free up more profit

Pitfall 24 A Reluctance to be Flexible

A lack of flexibility may be one of the biggest pitfalls for the new businessperson. You have meticulously planned you have researched and found evidence why your business will work, and you will succeed.

I doubt if any new business that went entirely to plan. The pitfall lies in getting too wedded to the plan you have created, pursuing regardless, investing more money and time while running off your forecast results are being missed.

In this issue actually lies the true nature of business. The world, the market, your customers and competitors are moving, the sands are shifting.

The differences in your results from those you forecast are called variances. Your first job is to measure these variances. If you know your variances and the trend they are creating, you can now move to your second job. Your second job is to assess whether these represent a major issue, or a blip or short term set back.

Statistically if you expected to win one out of every 5 quotations. You might be unlucky and lose the first 5 in a row but this in itself is not enough to be significant. Lose 10 in a row and you have a problem which should be urgently addressed. This is your third job, come up with solutions to problems with your strategy and plan. You will need to analyse the nature of this variance yourself.

Insufficient sales will force you to trim your costs and change something in your marketing approach. With every business I have run, I minimize my costs before I launched to protect against that sort eventuality.

That was a downside example but the upside, created by having too much success can also be problematic.

Imagine if you had won all 5 bids. This creates all manner of issues in resourcing and financing the work. Assess if this was a blip or if this is an issue with your plan. Are you under-pricing or offering too much for the money? You again have a problem to solve a good problem but still a problem. Do you instantly move to a bigger more aggressive model?

This can be a rough ride. I have had times when I ran myself ragged trying to cope with success with limited resources. Life seems wonderful but can be unsustainable in the longer term.

Either way, you are in for a roller coaster ride, enjoy the occasion, keep measuring and monitoring and you will survive. One lesson gleaned from numerous failures of small business is that putting 'good money after bad' has no future. You will arrive at the time to abandon. There is no shame in this, it is a prudent business decision. Ensure that you know why things went wrong and don't repeat them again.

Pitfall 25 A Failure to Align with your Suppliers

One aspect of business that many entrepreneurs fail to grasp or capitalize on is their relationship with suppliers and subcontractors. Because the relationship is often characterized by them wanting more money from you and you seek to minimize what you pay them, the relationship can become competitive rather than collaborative.

By failing to work together, you can become a less favoured customer and miss offers and opportunities they might access for you. When you are stuck and desperately need them to help-out they might be less inclined. Image you need to some parts or tools at a weekend and need the supplier to open his shop or warehouse as a favour to you. Will he rush out to help you or will he continue with his game of golf?

You and your supply chain compete with your competitors and their supply chain. Discuss collaboration and see what opportunities this opens up. Your supply chain stretches from your most basic parts or component or tool suppliers right through potentially to your logistics company who deliver your products.

Logistics is an area that illustrates this concept well. As consumers, we increasingly want next day or sometimes same day delivery. Companies now use this as a competitive edge. When I ran courses globally, I relied on my equipment suppliers and logistics companies to delivered course equipment to the course venue, to clear customs and ensure everything was in working condition, not damaged.

Course quality relied on not only my teaching but on the ancillary equipment, flip charts, pin-boards, pens, projectors and audio equipment. If there was a logistics problem I could not complain and moan to my client, I had to find a solution. I absolutely relied on having selected good suppliers and their ability to deliver to a high standard.

The best example I can point to is my father's business. He was the paint, glass and wallpaper wholesaler to Northern Scotland and the Islands. His business was an integral to his suppliers and his customers supply chain.

He would give expert advice to his customers on product use.

If a painter ran out of a wallpaper during a job, my father would source the paper himself or contact the manufacturer to use their entire customer base to source the right shade.

On jobs that his customers had that went wrong my father would do a site visit to identify and offer solutions to the problems.

My father would advise customers on what stock to buy for their shops. Trust became so high, in many of these relationships that customers would ask him to write his own order.

If a customer was left with an oversupply of stock, my father would buy it back.

It would be easy to say, these were different times. They were but I think this displayed professionalism and a recognition that good companies succeed by cooperating not competing along their supply chain. If you are skilled at this, you can create a competitive edge.

My consultancy used a world leading set of change tools. We on occasions sold courses led by the author of the tools, we trained and licensed others to use them. When we had questions, the author would advise us when needed over the phone. Our supply chains were so integrated that we actively looked for opportunities to collaborate.

By dedicating time to work together we both benefited to a high degree. I flew to America and stayed a week with him and his wife on a couple of occasions to learn more and to develop joint working arrangements. He visited me in Scotland. We travelled to Dubai, Chicago and London to jointly deliver programmes. Such cooperation makes for an enjoyable working relationship. Our clients loved this access to the author.

As another of my collaborators pointed out, when you enter self-employment you will miss the *company picnic*. In other word the enjoyment of working with other people. The best collaborative arrangements might give you this. A joiner might collaborate with a plumber and an electrician to their mutual benefit. She might collaborate with a kitchen designer and manufacturer. There are many ways to collaborate along the supply chain to mutual advantage.

Section Four Marketing and Sales

Marketing and Sales Essentials

Business Plan

Marketing Plan

Sales Funnel

Sales Pipeline

Business Plan

The start point for a new Business Marketing and Sales comes from the Business Plan as described in Section Three.

The Business Plan demonstrates how the business will succeed. Constructed at the outset you can produce a set of numbers which demonstrate how many items you might sell to whom and at what price. If you can use basic research to demonstrate that your numbers are a reasonable estimate, then you have a viable business.

In a manufacturing business, products will be costed in terms of raw materials, components and labour to establish their cost price to be balanced against the likely sales price.

The Business Plan then is developed into a Strategy, (see Pitfall 16) which provides the priorities of the business. Which products are preferred, which markets will have the most emphasis and which potential clients will be targeted? Where will work focus and given limited resources what will the business choose not to pursue.

From the Strategy a Marketing Plan is developed to become a part of the Operating Plan specifying what actions to take to deliver the sales figures forecast. The plan identifies allocates tasks in the sales and marketing process.

A one-person business also needs to undertake this activity. As time is much tighter detailed planning and forethought ought to make the use of that limited time much more productive.

From the Marketing and Sales elements of the Business Plan once finalized should emerge the Marketing Plan. A Marketing Plan addresses different aspects.

The Marketing Plan

Here are the headings that I used to create a Marketing Plan for this book. They are suitable for most types of Marketing Plan with minor adjustments. You could use them as slide headers or page headers for yours.

Marketing Objectives

Product

People

Place

Price

Position

Promotion

Package

Channels

Marketing Mix

Message

Competition

Marketing Budget

Strategy

Sales Funnel

Monetization

Marketing Plan

Research

Sales Funnel

The Funnel basically generates sales leads then moves them a step at a time until a sale is concluded. It is called a funnel because you gather large numbers of potential customers through the top. As the funnel narrows down you eliminate unlikely prospects. At the narrow bottom you arrive at successful sales.

Your Market Promotion approach whether email, tendering, digital advertising, mail shots or word of mouth is your prospecting process. Review which methods bring success and which do not. You can alter your approach to something that works better. Digital marketing permits trial and tests to invest monthly in advertising and then alter or change your approach. Traditional methods did not provide such flexibility.

The key concept to grasp is the *Funnel*. From first engagement, you improve the quality of your prospect so that you can invest face-to-face time or a telephone conversation, on those most likely to buy.

The best chances of getting a sale are in person conversations with well qualified prospects. This has always and will always be the best method of making high value sales.

In this digital age marketing automation is common by building a funnel attracting enquiries digitally from Social Media onto a landing page. From there prospects are further qualified, often by getting them to register for a personal marketing call. This can be efficient and economical allowing larger numbers of prospects to be targeted and rapidly narrowing them down to prime prospects. This approach makes presentation or telephone call time much more productive.

Qualifying prospects means checking, through your sales approach, how likely a prospect is to buy from you. In this way you ensure sales time is spent where most likely to generate sales and not wasted on unlikely contacts.

Finally, request a sale and conclude the deal. Many new business owners fail to grasp the importance of asking for someone to commit, they let the contact drift waiting for the prospect to say something. Make it easy for the prospect to say yes. Give them a choice where both answers are yes. Will I put you down for the red one or the blue one? Would you like us to start this week or next?

Learn about sales techniques online or from a book. Most importantly sell, sell, sell. Sales is something you will get better at the more that you do.

Your Funnel may be simpler. Advertise by flyer or local services listing - receive phone call - visit job - submit estimate - get job or not.

Sales Pipeline

From the Marketing Plan comes the actions to implement the plan. These Marketing and Sales stages are captured in the Sales Pipeline. The pipeline lists all leads generated. The Pipeline includes the name of the customer, the estimated value of the work, the dates the work is expected to be done. Against each lead the stage the lead has reached in the process is recorded: Discussing, Scoping. Tender received, preparing to bid, bid submitted, negotiating. The next column captures the result, won, lost, negotiating, postponed.

Some more complex pipelines include a probability of winning work. e.g., 100% if you are certain the work is yours, versus 10% for a remote chance.

When I worked in the diving industry the bulk of our work came from substantial tender processes. We expected to win 1 in 5 or a 20% success rate which coincidentally was about the same in management consultancy.

This enabled me to make a reasonable forecast of what income we might expect to generate over time I.e. If we tendered for 15 jobs at an average of $500k each. I could forecast that we might win 3 of these generating approximately $1.5 million.

I could place this income across a number of months and would be able to see if this was on plan or if we required to find more work.

This Pipeline allows you to forecast the future income you can expect. The pipeline also permits you to review what is happening and improve your results in the future. For example, I developed niche client areas where we would win 100% of the work.

I use an Excel spreadsheet to keep my pipeline in every business. It is very simple within everybody's ability to create.

Analysis of the pipeline reveals:

Which adverting method worked.

How many jobs won or lost and why?

These simple metrics allow you to improve your chances of success, marketing investment and advertising methods. They demonstrate whether your pricing is too high or inadequate.

Pitfall 26 Limited Product Lines

This section is really about creating multiple income streams. There are three good reasons for having multiple income streams.

First: Multiple income streams provide diversity of income where the different streams offer different rates of growth and different success rates.

Second: A single income stream is a risk if for any reason that stream ceases to be viable.

Third: Multiple streams provide the opportunity to increase your income through related products and services.

My podcast plan is an example. On top of advertising revenue my main income source; I realized I could provide a number of other related products and services, that would increase my income.

Income Diversity

In my example, my core income was planned to come from advertising but recognizing the limitations I added sponsorship as a second income source. I also decided to use the materials I created in alternative income streams. The first of these you are reading in the form of this book. The book I am writing is associated with a further income stream I am offering in the form of on-line coaching, mentoring and Business Plan review and assistance. As the podcast plan has been relegated the book and coaching have become my focus.

In my first consultancy business my original plan was to do Procurement Consultancy. I diversified to also offer meeting facilitation which I was trained to do enjoyed and had experienced of.

Facilitation income soon superseded my procurement income.

Facilitation was then replaced with much larger consultancy projects interspersed with running training courses which also became a lucrative source of income. Later still consultancy programs for foreign government departments also did well.

You can see how at different times the emphasis changed but by keeping avenues open and building my resources and skills and confidence I kept my business growing and delivering profits. This also kept my interest up. I love variety but focus on delivering the best job on the focus that I have on hand. Brainstorm what your different income streams might be.

Often you build a business over time. You find synergies, opportunities and connections to the skills and experience that you have. By working with your customers and clients they identify opportunities for you to do more to support them and fulfil their needs. This becomes an immensely rewarding aspect of your business life.

Risk Management

Exposure of a single product to risk is important. Imagine a product business losing a legal challenge for a breach of copyright. That business would be finished. Markets can change with legislation or new innovative market entrants.

Additional Income and Profit

One business I coached provided short videos for commercial clients and clubs.

We identified, video hosting and streaming as an additional income stream. The provision of stock footage, motion graphics, creation of web versions for social media, increased the potential income for each job by almost 50%.

This makes a difference to a small business and these services were delivered using existing suppliers and software they had already bought so every additional service provided additional profit at zero additional expense.

The combination of these income streams and diversity can make your business more secure, more profitable and open opportunities you might never originally have conceived of.

Diversification can have drawbacks. Diversification ought not to be so much as to lose focus on the core of your business. Diversification ought not to become running two businesses at once as neither might succeed. Training and Consultancy sat well together as we often provided these in parallel with each other or using one to advance a client's objectives in the other.

On a consultancy restructuring an Oil Company, we trained facilitators to support the process. We facilitated the leadership meetings and trained managers in change to better understand implementation of the organisation changes we had proposed.

These additional services doubled the original contract value. The training course continued for years beyond the end of the original consultancy projects.

Multiple business lines work best when they are complimentary with each other. This also deepens the relationship with the client and opens up additional opportunities. The Consultancy and Training also led in time to a Leadership Coaching contract. Synergy works well provided there is no conflict of interest which is an issue to be aware of.

Pitfall 27 A Failure to Develop Your Product

Products and services need taken from idea to reality. This can be a long and difficult process. The first step is to flesh out a design on paper.

In the case of a Product next comes the prototype stage. There are companies who specialize in making these prototypes. Prototypes can be dummies which show the look of a product or in some cases a full working example. Prototyping allows a product to be tested and researched without going into a full production test.

Prototypes allow more detailed production planning and costing. The prototype allows manufacturers to estimate the cost and time for production of tens or thousands of the product. A more careful examination of any health and safety or regulatory issues become possible.

Some products require more than others. A car for example requires destructive crash testing and numerous safety tests. Making several prototypes which will be destroyed is a big cost and explains why so many small manufacturers went out of the car business. When EU product testing was applied to e-cigarettes the number of suppliers drastically dropped as each product line tested required an expenditure of £50,000!

If you deliver a service rather than a physical product, a testing or trial phase is important. A window cleaner starts by offering the service to family and friends to measure how long cleaning each window takes. This is a critical piece of information for costing a job. He might compare the effectiveness of different ladders and cleaning products and supplies allowing better estimation of how the business works in practice.

The next stage is to look at protecting your product so that your idea cannot be stolen or copied. This can be done by applying for copyright or other forms of intellectual property rights. This is an expensive process involving a firm of solicitors or copyright agents specializing in this area of law.

The first check ensures that the idea has not been registered by someone else. You then decide on the geography in which you wish to protect your idea. Your own country, countries over the world part of various treaties to mutually protect copyright. Finally, specific non-treaty countries. Each area requires more money to register and perform the searches.

Ideas that require substantial investment will need to be protected in the appropriate geography. No prudent investor will put money into an unprotected idea.

Global copyright protection is expensive. Remember that having the protection still requires you to investigate and prosecute breaches of your copyright.

Pitfall 28 A Failure to Understand your Market

Too often enthusiasm for an exciting idea overtakes the reality of what the market will support. Watch a few episodes of TV programmes like Dragons Den if you need to proof of this.

Markets can be researched to identify who your clients and customers might be. How many of them exist?

For local businesses finding numbers of people living within your catchment is easily searched online. Deeper analysis will give their ages and social groupings which ought to provide sound base statistics for food businesses, tradesmen and other high street enterprises. A key skill is to take data and convert that data into something useful for assessing your business idea. Developing this takes time but is not difficult.

Example

You want to open a Bar and are interested in what your potential customer base might be.

Your town has a population of 10,000 and no other bars. For this example, I will not include food which many bars use to increase footfall and profits.

Q1. How many adults are of drinking age? Say 80% of people are over 18 so 8,000 people.

Q2. How many of these people drink? I researched this online and found a figure of 20% increasing annually. Let's say 25% for business planning purposes which gives 2,000 potential customers.

Q3. How many people drink only at home? I found two bits of solid statistical reports, a government one and one by 'Drink Aware'. From the Drink Aware statistics, I discovered 34% of drink is consumed in licensed premises and £7.20 a week was the average spend. I can change this in my calculations by judging how affluent my area is. I can visit similar pubs and see how much is being spent by their patrons over an evening. Research can be enjoyable.

By taking 5300 customers (66%) of drinkers I might have identified my target market. Many home drinkers also drink in pubs, but I will use 66% as my starting point.

Q4. What percentage of UK adults are non-drinkers? An internet search suggested 21% from reliable figures. This eliminates a further 1100 potential customers. Leaving me with 4200 customers, excluding those coming for a soft drink who may offer a different an opportunity.

I have to make deductions for those who go out with my town to drink which realistically is probably the same number that might travel to drink in my bar so no change in my estimates. Factor in those who for whatever reason will not frequent my bar.

I estimate that 50% of my potential market are never likely to enter my pub as it is just not their thing. This immediately deducts 2100 from my potential customer numbers, leaving 2100. Say 2000 for this example.

Q5. How many times a week will customers visit my bar?

This is the most difficult figure to estimate. Most TV soaps would have you imagine everyone is there daily. I devised this idea thinking of people that I know:

Regulars 5% twice a week = 200 visits a week

Irregulars 20% twice a month - 200 visits a week

Occasional 40% once a quarter – 67 visits a week

Others 30% once a year – 15 a week

Estimated visits = 482 patrons a week

I would want to access industry figures before proceeding. Most people buy existing bars thus knowing the turnover and footfall in advanced. If I think about my local there are usually 10-40 people in there a night, that in a town of 3000 inhabitants. The number of customers in a local bar might be related to clubs using it, sports leagues and other group use.

Usage is seasonal with the Christmas period accounting for largest numbers. Local holidays, fairs and festivals also boost numbers.

If they spend the average £7.20 each that would give £3470 as my weekly turn over - £180,000 a year. I read excellent busy bars in affluent areas will turnover more than £7000 a week. So, I can take a view. Either pessimistic or optimistic on which to develop my business model.

Now you can see how I arrived at useable figures by creating the questions I needed answering and finding reliable data to respond to these. I completed the above forecast using just one of these sources my next step of course would be to cross-check these with other sources.

I generated this as an example of how I would attempt to generate some numbers for my business plan. Do I think these are accurate? Probably not. I would need a better source of numbers to finalise my plan, but I would have something to compare these against which might allow me to take a view on the quality and reliability of my numbers.

I would also take account of the big picture where the number of pubs closing is increasing rapidly in the UK.

Having generated these figures, take a view on how accurate a representation they are. A single pub in a 10,000 catchment without competition is a rarity. My figure is a starting point for preparing a plan.

As a business, I would have ideas for increasing visits and spend per head to succeed.

Can my business survive on £3470 revenue a week? This depends on my overheads cost of the beer, your income, wine and spirits, rent, staff, insurance, business rates and other costs. Given the cost of the stocks of alcohol these numbers are not optimistic as a business as they stand. This is a rough example. I would speak to several bar owners before going any further.

What might I need to do to increase my numbers? Ought I to target my idea on a better area? This is not a process that requires any particular skill just one that needs some detailed work and a realistic attitude.

WARNING: The internet is notorious for delivering bad information. The most reliable data comes from government databases which are accessible and free as well as paid for marketing sector analysis.

Overestimating your market or how successful your promotions/advertising might be fatal flaws that hit a new business hard and early. An example is business promoted by the use of mail or email. You might think your product is great and desirable but success rates from such advertising can be less than 2% traditionally.

The marketing ideas of new businesses are fraught with wrong assumptions about what people buy, why, when and how. Customers tend to go for people and products they know so new businesses are at a disadvantage.

Fortunately, newer forms of online advertising can be more finely focussed on your target customer. To do this you understand who that target customer is.

When starting a business, write down who your number one customer would be.

What age are they?

What sex?

Where do they live?

What is their employment?

What income do they earn?

Why would they buy your product or service?

By going through this exercise, you will reveal your own prejudices as well as insight into your wider client base. Now can you calculate how many of this type of customer exists and of course how they will find out about your business and how you could best contact them.

Pitfall 29 Working with Bad Customers

Customers exist that you do not want. When launching a Business, you chase every opportunity, even those that you secretly have a bad feeling about. Customers can promise the earth for the future. They take help and advice without paying, they monopolize your time. They are demanding, they pay late or don't pay at all. These Customers damage your business, and they make you feel bad about yourself.

How did I allow myself to get into this position? I ignored the issues that I believed existed.

Some customers who give you work and pay are also too much of a problem. They drain your time and your energy, they upset your staff.

A small IT start-up I coached had too many of these. Small businesses tend in the early stages to have other small businesses as customers. Cash is tight, they administer themselves badly, they under price and damage the market. My client's solution was to create a process they called 'sacking customers'. They passed them onto a much larger hosting company for which they received an affiliate fee. Knowing they whilst their clients would get professional service the larger company the large company would not accept the nonsense that they were put through and the customer would not attempt it.

They then focussed their time and effort on clients who worked with them not against them. The good clients received a more focussed service and were delighted, paid promptly and asked for more work as they grew with their service. My clients were happy and relaxed in their work.

Many times, your only option is to walk away. Not looking to the longer term is always hard. Is this a customer that helps or harms your long-term prospects? Ignore promises of future work completely unless tangible proof shows it is real. A bad customer is a often a bad supplier to their customers and their long-term prospects are fatally flawed.

Look for the signs. If they complain of staff and customer problems these are signs to pick up on. If promises are broken beware. just say:

"Thank you for the opportunity but I don't think we are the right company to help you." Not starting beats weeks of anguish. Listen to that inner voice warning you that all is not right.

Do not be the bad customer yourself. One that gets pulled into a situation where paying bills is a problem and who breaks off communications because of embarrassment.

Confront situations head on, is the only way to work. If a problem occurs inform those involved promptly, they might even have suggestions to help. I had a contractor who was taking longer to deliver than planned. I noticed he was doing work for others during this period. He suggested he might be unable to complete my work. I invited him in for a chat.

It turned out that he was not getting enough income from my work hence the other work. I offered to make milestone payments on evidence of completed work. This solved his problem, and he was able to move on with my work to my complete satisfaction. I am sure the episode gave him great anxiety. If he had brought the issue to my attention, I could have relieved this problem without hesitation. I am sure that he learnt from the episode.

Pitfall 30 A Reluctance to Sell

I have coached many individuals who were planning to leave big companies to start their own business. Common to this group is a single fatal flaw and that is a reluctance to sell. No business or indeed employment in any industry or size of organisation that does not require selling skills. You sell yourself to a new employer, you sell your ideas to your peers. But when it comes to with lifting the phone or knocking on someone's door, Selling seems to be a dirty word.

Their mental model is flawed. These individuals tell themselves; selling is embarrassing, demeaning or in some ways embarrassing or strange. We all buy and so recognise the requirement for someone to be doing the selling to us. Too many examples exist of selling being miscalled which lead to the flawed model. Estate Agents for example are ridiculed yet most are professional and fair. Market traders have a stereotype, yet most are helpful and entertaining.

The challenge is not just a reluctance to sell in person a new trend is that everything can be done digitally. E-commerce, Social Media Google AdWords. You can run business online however at some point creating relationships with real people will become important.

At the root of this lies a fear of rejection. What if someone I contact does not want my product? We are aware that only a small percentage of potential buyers will buy. By selling we are working outhouse who don't want to buy!

A reluctance to sell and to build personal relationships with your customers will be terminal to your business eventually.

Just do It! Give yourself a talking to. You are providing great products or valuable services that will benefit your customers. Now get out and sell with pride. Only by physically selling will you learn how to sell and get over any inhibitions. The theorists will say a fear of rejection underpins a reluctance to sell. Do so much selling that rejection is common but success is all the more pleasant.

A lot depends on the experience you have had in your youth. As well as the examples I cite elsewhere, I did bob-a-job with the boy scouts, I sold Christmas cards. I worked at boy scout fetes on a book stall and I sold lots of things in lots of circumstances.

I suggest elsewhere the business model for a market stall. If you are confident about going into business but selling is a challenge, perhaps you should open a stall for a few days as a learning exercise.

Car boot sales are a perfect opportunity to try out your sales skills. A weekend invested in this is invaluable and possibly profitable and beats any corporate training.

I have a close friend who is a very successful businessman who owns a substantial company. He spends every weekend on a stall at a farmer's market selling produce from his son's business. He sells because he really enjoys the whole experience, the selling, bartering, exchanging with other traders and interacting with the public. Can you imagine selling for enjoyment, a hobby? In his own business he is, the best salesman I ever met.

Try this, make selling your new passion and if every sale is a joy imagine how your business will grow. Get out and sell, sell, sell your way to success.

You can have the greatest Marketing and Sales Strategy in the world, but a strategy only delivers when it is effectively implemented.

A move to communicate more digitally has arisen in the modern world.

Key to your business success is engaging with customers. People buy from people still remains the rule.

Yesterday I watched a video by a successful American online entrepreneur. She shared that whist she created leads online collecting telephone numbers and speaking with potential clients brought in the bulk of her income and profit.

Many new businesses get online and trust that customers will find them and buy. That is not reality. Create a close relationship and you win a customer for life. Customers enjoy doing business with suppliers they like.

Engagement is a Communication process. I will share my process with you. For your own purposes you might need to modify this approach, but the same logic applies.

Objective

The first part of the Process of a conversation with a prospective client is to identify the Objective from the engagement. It might be as simple as getting work or selling a product or setting up a tender to win a big project. Before going to any client meeting, write 1-3 short objectives to achieve from the meeting and a note of what you think the client most needs. I will repeat that – find out what your client needs as your priority. Your customer needs must come first in a sales conversation.

Influences

The next stage is to consider the influences impacting a potential customer's decisions. If you are contacting a business question 1 is: 'Where are they in their budgeting process?' There is no point chasing work if a company has neither the money nor the approval to spend it. You can set yourself up to be included in their future spending plans of course. Consider their strategy are you a fit with how they work? How do you find these things out? You ask them, as simple as that.

Influences shape how a prospective customer hears your Message.

Channels

Having identified a suitable client identify the right channels to market to them. Should you phone them, try to get an appointment, what other channels be appropriate. The more significant the opportunity the more personal the channel ought to be.

Message

The final part of engagement is to design the message you are giving to your client. This might be how you describe your service or product; this might be a brochure or some other form of communication. You should not rely solely on them reading your material be prepared to follow up in person.   Be aware that everything you do in delivering your message is a part of your message. Be professional, be prompt, and prepared.

A simple process with practice you will excel at.

Decision Makers

For marketing purposes, understand who makes decisions. The Project Manager may be a friend but if their boss makes the decision, you need to develop the relationship with her.

Who Builds?

By looking at these priorities I can establish who in my company is best suited to establish the relationship. This is not merely matching each level in my client with the same level in my organisation but rather the most appropriate person to build an effective relationship to make the sale.

Pitfall 31 An Over Reliance on the Web

Many young entrepreneurs have been brought up with the internet age. The web appears to offer access to a world of consumers and opportunity. Appropriately used the web opens up new avenues to markets. As your marketing and sales tool there are limitations.

The internet appears to be a free to use super resource to access your clients and promote your business at a competitive cost.

Like traditional marketing, web sales take real expertise to skilfully utilize the internet and its many tools. Many tools getting pushed at you.

Providing information on using the internet to gain business is in itself a huge business. Amongst this hordes of promoters and promotional tools an interesting phenomenon can be detected. A disproportionate number of companies promoting ranking and sales tools for purchase. Think about this for a second. If someone was so great at achieving internet sales success, they would surely create a web shop themselves to make their fortune. This is typical of many online tools and sales services.

Reliance on a website may be a catastrophic mistake. Over 650 million active web sites are currently online. To rely on your website being found in this mass of digital content is poor practice unless you are prepared to budget for real expertise to ensure your site ranks well and achieves its objectives.

Selecting a digital supplier, you will require a personal recommendation and not just select one of the thousands of random offerings.

The same applies to advertising on social media. Many platforms are available to you but choosing the right ones requires you to set a budget and chose the right tool and method to get to your clients. Again, expertise counts, and the digital domain is full of well-meaning amateurs and its fair number of less well-meaning incompetents.

Social Media ought to be a part of your business strategy but can absorb hours of your valuable time for little or no return.

A top digital marketing company can be expensive given you pay for their input and the advertising, but the best can make a dramatic impact on your results. The web can be everything your business needs but be prepared to spend to get the right partner.

Search for someone with expertise who can demonstrate successes achieved and provide real references and case studies who you can talk to about their service. As with any promotion, seek advice from your chosen expert, with their help; set a budget, test your approach for a period to see if that approach delivers you value. If not think again.

Beware of relying on optimistic sales figures claimed to be achieved through the world wide web.

To an extent using the web to target local business works well. The costs are appropriate and well targeted protects your time bringing in contactable contacts without diluting these with contacts offering no prospect of business.

Pitfall 32 A Failure to Track Competition

I learnt this at the diving company I worked for. We had 100% of the largest offshore construction company's business and at the highest rates in the industry which was an expensive business.

How did we achieve this? Our divers were exceptional, and the only ones employed on a full-time contract in an industry which used daily contract divers. We built and supplied high quality superior dive systems for every one of our client's vessels. We only charged when the vessel was on hire. If the client needed an additional system, we built one at huge cost. We understood our client's business and did

everything we could to ensure their success.

Our competitors offered our client to mimic our model and undercut our prices on a yearly basis but so aligned were our businesses that our client always politely declined, and we kept the business.

Section Five Operations and Administration

Operations Framework

To be operationally efficient and effective you would expect to see:

An Operating Plan

A scoping process to identify the separate tasks and resources to complete a piece of work

A methodology for scheduling and resourcing work

A Costing Process

Commercial processes for Tendering and Contracting

Operating Plan

Operations is the area which is the starting point for most businesses. You start out to be a painter and decorator so painting and decorating is what you do.

This is the most fluid of your plans and the plan changes constantly in its detail.

In simple terms Operations is the work the business and its departments or personnel do, or you do yourself! The Operating Plan comprises the key tasks which deliver the Business Plan via your strategy.

Tasks are scheduled. Leadership tasks are schedule in advance whilst workforce tasks emerge during the year and are scheduled as work is won.

The Strategy guides the prioritization of different tasks.

Every employee has his or her role and responsibilities to guide every task they undertake once allocated.

Most organizations allocate tasks and responsibilities for management and supervisory staff which are planned and allocated in the Operations Plan.

Execution of the Operating Plan ought to deliver the Objectives of the Business.

Your operation planning has two sets of actions to resource and schedule:

First there is the work you win which should take the bulk of your time and resources.

Second there are business activities outside the actual work. This would include sales activities, stock purchase, shelf stacking and stock taking, finance activities such as keeping accounts and sending invoices. Preparing proposals and prices for future work. Maintenance of your plant and equipment. The seemingly endless list of activity running a professional business requires.

The Operating Plan addresses the number of resources required to deliver these forecasts. Put simply how many employees might be required of what skill levels and experience and at what times? If you are a self-employed tradesman what tools do you need? If you are doing a lot of work, what items might you need more than one of?

Scaffolding is an example. Scaffolding is often hired not owned. If you owned the scaffolding poles and fittings you might require two sets to give time for erection and dismantling. Put simply with several concurrent jobs dismantling and erecting scaffolds every day would be inefficient.

To maximize your own personal resources, you need a way to manage competing demands on your time and equipment. Who and what gets priority? When do you fit in marketing and administration activities?

Scope

When doing your estimate, quotation or tender you will itemize the resources required to complete the work. In this way you can manage your resources and ensure that you keep to the program and consequently manage costs.

Scheduling

Every job has to be scheduled to fit in to the available time. Scheduling for one person ought to be relatively straightforward. Do you have capacity time to do something in your schedule? Arranging jobs to ensure continuous work may need more complex decision-making.

If you undertake larger jobs and start employing or subcontracting other tradesmen, resourcing work becomes more difficult and keeping a continuous flow of work more important.

In terms of process and documentation a diary or planner might be sufficient, on paper or digitally depending on your personal preferences. I like to see things graphically so large wall planners are my favoured tool for scheduling.

Execute, Review and Adjust

To complete the work, review and adjust is the problem-solving process you will be familiar with. You call this juggling your time!

Learn

The last step ought to be to learn if your scheduling system is working efficiently.

How many customers complain, 'They started the job, went away and took days to come back and complete the work.' We are aware that this is a scheduling and time management issues. An Operations problem. The better you learn the less that this happens.

I employed a joiner, to fit some bifold doors. He installed the doors, but several small tasks were incomplete: replacing the render, sealing the gap below the door ledge and removing the old doors from site. This took three further visits each of which required a car journey and travel time for at most half an hour of work. He lost his profit margin in these unnecessary extra trips.

Pitfall 33 A Failure to Give Time to your Objectives

The process of scheduling, resourcing and doing the work of the business is separate from the process of creating an Operating Plan to action your Objectives.

The biggest issue many small and medium-sized businesses face is a failure to convert objectives into purposeful action. Without action nothing happens. Once you established what you want to achieve these Objectives need converting into a plan.

Your plan has three distinct sections:

Part One: Work Plans. The work to be completed and allocation of

resources, people and equipment to that work. If the business is just you, allocate the time you require allocated to every task to complete.

Part Two: Business Development. Many additional actions are required to make your business successful. These will include product development and marketing against your Objectives and resources need to be allocated to complete these. You generate these in your Marketing Plan.

Part 3 Administration activities. These are in the form of a diary listing the admin tasks to be done. I will work all night if necessary, to ensure these tasks are done on time and when scheduled. These are less detailed tasks. These activities take the form of reminders to do actions well on time to avoid getting fines and warnings for late submissions of legal requirements like submitting annual accounts. For example, submit Companies House return, submit accounts, renew insurance.

These 3 Plans are quite separate.

Different types of business adopt different formats but for illustration the following is how I approached this.

For Part 1, draft a Project Plan that itemizes the work and the hours, individuals and time to complete these. For complex work a planner like Microsoft Project is used. Smaller companies or sole traders might use a wall planner or big diary.

For the Part 2 plan.

To put Objectives into action, follow this approach:

Write out my Objectives and identify 3-4 key things which must be achieved to hit that Objective.

Example

1. Increase turnover to £1Million a year (Objective)

Gain 4 new £ 3k clients a week (Sub-Objective)

Contact 50 prospective clients each week (Action)

Speak to Digital Marketing expert End February (Action)

Set up a Facebook advert targeted at new customers by end March (Action)

You can see the idea. Do the same for 6-12 Objectives. Sub-Objectives become the Plan. The Actions, which will be at least 18-50, prioritized, are the means by which Objectives are achieved. The actions themselves are now plugged into monthly, weekly or daily things to do lists. Focus a things-to-do list on the 3-4 things that move the business on most. Under each Objective write the detailed actions to do against each of these sub points.

Write the dates these must be achieved by and place them into the plan. Review these to ensure that you allocate enough time bearing in mind the activity in part one of the plan. It is too easy to be excited by Objectives and underestimate the time required or the reality of time available given the conflicting priorities.

Review the Part One Plan weekly.

The Part Two Plans sets monthly, weekly and daily to do lists.

For the Part 3 plan: Keep a dedicated diary with due dates to remind you of the important administration activities. Ensure that activities which take time to complete have a reminder to start these well in advance of the due date.

The Part 3 diary is referred to weekly but is not time consuming if you keep on top of it.

Pitfall 34 A Failure of Governance

The quality of your work becomes an essential element of your future success. Your reputation ensures future work and demand. This becomes more difficult if you employed others as your reputation relies on their quality not just your own work. This introduces the need for inspection of their work, training and development of their skills and rectification of anything not up to standard.

Health and Safety

Issues of Health and Safety of yourself, staff, clients and their property and the public coming in contact with your work, also fall within operations. Industry requirements, legislative requirements all are to be followed and complied with. Health and Safety culture has its critics but in the end accidents, failures and breaches cost a disproportionate amount of money and time so justify the effort to prevent these.

Whether you are in construction trades, catering or financial services or indeed any business there will be H.S.E. implications to be covered especially when you employ others.

Studying industry literature and joining industry bodies will give an awareness of rules and regulations which impact your business. This includes the signage you must display in your premises and at sites. Not knowing these will not be a defence of any legal action against you following an incident or accident.

Pitfall 35 A Failure to take The Right Action

My most common diagnosis for Business failure has been a failure to take the correct actions. Everyone says they are prepared to do 'everything it takes' to be successful. The issue is twofold.

Some, mean by this, everything it takes except.... others will do 'everything' it takes just not enough of it to reach the tipping point between success and failure.

Identify what it is that makes the difference in your business and take action and keep taking action all the way to success. Many new businesses spend their time in planning, designing and developing, new products, web sites, brochures. Too often these are not the things that make a difference. Be aware of what makes a difference in your business.

Many young entrepreneurs succeed where smarter more experienced ones fail. The difference I believe is a willingness to take action. Put aside any fears and misgivings and act. The right action is what pays. When I am writing, the right action is to write and to edit. Once written and published the right action is to promote, the book. If you are in product sales, the action is most probably to sell, sell and sell. The right action is often the action you find yourself reluctant or nervous to do.

The flip side of this is an addiction to the wrong action. I worked with individuals who used *busy work* to avoid doing the right things. They made the cleverest and most spectacular slide presentations, they built databases, they tidied cupboards, anything to avoid the right action. Even in the largest companies these individuals exist. This is a character trait that does not work in your own business.

One typical failing is to think that additional training or qualifications is the same as growing your business. Wrong! Training in my experience can be an avoidance activity. Individuals who enjoy attending training are most often those who dislike sales and marketing.

In business some actions are much more important than others. These are the critical actions that lead to our success. The right action is often the most difficult, so most imaginatively avoided, modified or mitigated. in a multi-level-marketing business the critical action is to call people, to invite them to view the opportunity or the products.

Identify early the key actions to grow your business. These actions address the business drivers impacting volume of business, sales. Number of customers, quality of service reduction of costs. These will differ from business to business.

Remember my story about the diving company I worked for owned by a multi-millionaire who phoned once a week and asked only one question. "How many divers are contracted now? He knew that this influenced, number of clients, turnover and profitability. This information was enough for him. When these numbers failed to meet his expectations he flew in, met with key clients and potential new clients, and then he flew home. He ran the entire business around doing the right action.

What is your key Business driver? What action most influences this? In the diving company the business driver was number of contracted divers. We achieved this by marketing to secure more tenders and bidding to win more work the process that sold divers.

The whole company focussed on this, with everyone aligned behind the effort. It took hard work and long hours. I recall the M.D. At 4am photocopying bids being directed by the junior marketing secretary. Why? That is what it required to get done on time.

Sufficiently Resourced Actions

The second essential is that the big actions are resourced in terms of time. Poorly timed actions and goals allow them to be overlooked and resources moved elsewhere on to other less significant tasks.

Imagineering

I used to facilitate key meetings for big clients. The final step would be to identify and allocate actions. Everyone would be excited and often a 'macho' attitude to taking on actions arose.

Learn to rehearse all the important actions asking the action owner or indeed yourself:

Describe the steps required to complete the action?

Is this able to be resourced to meet the agreed deadline?

Is the timescale correct?

Will you be able to resource this given your other priorities?

Given that that reassess the commitment of time required.

Are there any requests of others to ensure this action is delivered on time?

I describe this as Imagineering the process of conceptualizing actions as we commit.

Enough is the Enemy of Success.

Going back to the Multi-level Marketing business. The organisation taught, 12 contacts were required to arrange 3 prospects to meet and 1 to sign up. Distributors set themselves an action to contact 12 people a week. some found contacting difficult, but would do 11 or 12, often not the best prospects, but be happy that they had made the goal. This was successful but on reflection nonsense.

Why set a limit on how many contacts to make. Why stop at 12? because they arbitrarily decided that is '*enough*' to complete the action? Calls took less than 5 minutes but anticipating them took much longer. Resourcing these is not difficult an hour a week for 12. When distributors could find an hour a night!

By keeping going past 12 and on to 20 or 30 or more.

That would have:

Increased successful results

Allowed focus on serious prospects

Demonstrated to those who joined what worked

Overcome fears of contacting

Created momentum and excitement. This is fundamental the right key action well-resourced and actively pursued until final success.

Massive Action

The importance of taking such action to ensure success and momentum is difficult to understate. Too much success is always easier to manage than too little.

Massive action ensures not falling foul of the barriers to action which are distraction and avoidance. Distraction occurs when something else takes our interest and enthusiasm and diverts us from our direction. Avoidance is when we fear the consequences of our actions. Become expert at catching yourself avoiding the actions you must take.

Contacting prospective customers is a common example:

What will people think of me?

What if they say no?

No one ever failed from someone saying 'no'. Keep going until 1000 people have said no, reward yourself then start again. Concentrate on those who said 'yes'.

These fears are purely imagined and as such your story in your mind can be changed. They are saying 'no' to their own success, they are saving your time by not engaging you. the process is one of finding those who say, 'Yes please'!

At times when I am feeling creative, I want to do things that are not necessarily moving the business forward.

If you maintain a To-Do-List and my advice is, you do. Always do the most important things on the list first.

Three lists are helpful.

Do today

Do later

Don't do ever

This focusses your important and urgent actions on today. The other two list allow you to park things and clear your day without getting diverted. These actions once written down do not need to occupy brain-space.

At one point when progress was slow, I used to choose the most important 3 items on the to do list every day and do just them every day. These were the items that most effectively moved my business forward

Pitfall 36 Over Working / Over delivering

These are two linked issues that can undermine a business from the start. You are getting paid for the work that you do. You enjoy your work. You charge, and customers pay. You are living your perfect life.

Your response is work harder and longer to deliver more. You are a perfectionist, wanting to justify your charges and your client's faith in you. You are working more than 8 hours a day, every day, working to improve and perfect every job. You work weekends, holidays, nights.

Overdelivering with overworking is unsustainable in the long term. You cannot deliver 5-star work at 2-star prices as the extra hours not paid for will harm your business. You will be forced to either reduce the quality or increase the prices. Once started this is hard unless demand for your goods and services is increasing.

Understand a few key elements here:

Work ideally should be done in the working week 8 - 12 hours a day with most weekends off. I understand that being self-employed needs long hours to meet your client's needs. This can be unsustainable over time, and everyone needs to be rested to recover and be refreshed.

Rates are appropriate for a particular standard of work delivered. Over delivering is fine but in the long term requires to be at higher prices or at least prices that match the effort. If your rates are fair, do not feel that you need to deliver 'extras' beyond those included in your rates.

By cutting prices you may win a lot more work. The extra hours will be a burden and you will not generate enough cash to prop the business up when things go wrong.

Pitfall 37 A Failure to Manage Reputation

One of the most substantial pitfalls a new business faces is loss of reputation. Reputation is hard won and can only be earned over time but can be lost considerably faster. The rate at which reputation is lost can be even faster in this digital age. Bad reviews spread far, and fast on Social Media.

Managing your reputation is as important as managing your Finances.

Where do you go first to find a new supplier? The internet. If you work with the internet, web site or social media you have a reputation to manage.

Do you buy after checking reviews? How many others do the same? The largest of businesses make a big point of encouraging reviews. Online complaints trigger instant responses and most large organizations employ dedicated staff monitoring channels like Twitter and Facebook. If you have a spare hour and want a laugh Google 'bad hotel reviews on Trip Adviser'.

These are amusing when they are about other peoples' businesses, not so, if they are about yours. Every bit of feedback you receive is useful if not always welcome. Some reviews are downright malicious.

Every client interaction is an opportunity to improve your service and encourage your customer to recommend you to others.

Whatever marketing and sales strategy you adopt, nothing beats personal recommendation. If we are looking for a tradesman, friends recommendations carry substantial weight. When you are having problems with a supplier or contractors a group of friends or neighbours share these problems and reputations are destroyed. One of our neighbours has had ongoing problems with a builder. The next time I am with them I will ask; 'How are things going with your house refitting?' Another neighbour is getting new windows, I would ask the same of them.

One bad review outweighs ten good ones.

I remember the excellent company that installed a skylight for us. We asked for a quote to do some more work, and they will win the work without doubt. We told no more than 3 of our friends about this company and only because the subject came up in conversation. People discuss problems more than the things that go well.

This ought to demonstrate that you protect your reputation at source. Respond promptly and politely, check that the customer is happy. Do the work professionally. Communicate. Keep the client advised on timing, delays and issues. If you keep communications live your clients don't speculate about what is or is not going on. Relationships built with your customers pay future dividends.

Pitfall 38 The Monster Within

The most difficult opponent to struggle with in your business is yourself. Now I am not pointing the finger, I am guilty of this. We all develop ingrained mental models which generate problems that we repeat. In given circumstances our behaviour is predictable. In time with effort, you can recognise these traits which are unhelpful to your business. We also possess positive traits which we can develop.

Identify these as, good habits, bad habits and omissions. We all display these and by surfacing these we control them.

Stop doing things that are unhelpful to your success. Do the things that work well and that you need to do more of. Why would any of us not follow these simple steps? We understand that this is hard!

Pitfall 39 Poor Time Management

One of the fundamental pillars of launching a new business is to understand and create a sustainable time management model. The most valuable resource that you as owner manage is time. For many of us our first proper business came after a few years of being in employment. Working 5 days a week, 9 to 5 with 2 - 4 weeks holiday a year.

I was extremely fortunate to create a model that worked when I started my first major Consultancy:

I worked two paid days a week generating over £100k turnover a year, providing procurement consultancy and facilitating client meetings and events. You may be thinking Whoopee! That's the model for me.

The other three days in the week were used to generate and manage the two chargeable client facing days. I spent time creating training courses, installing and updating anti-virus software and a host of other management tasks. I did marketing, prepared and followed up meetings and did a lot of travelling.

This is a productive model; I was VERY careful with overheads which I kept small. I replaced my expensive company car with a medium-sized economical family saloon. I often worked evenings and weekends to make this lifestyle sustainable. I tried hard to make time on a Friday to take my wife to our local pub for lunch. I took a few weeks off at Christmas my favourite time of year.

This created a sustainable lifestyle. By not being greedy, and not extravagant, I enjoyed my life and spent time with my family.

Gradually, demand for my time increased, I employed subcontractors to work with me and even increased my rates. Clients remained loyal, and I supported them.

Over 5 years this increased, and I enjoyed the rewards, but I was flying long haul at least once a week, rising at 5 am, working to 8pm. My life was rushing about, fitting the family around a hectic schedule as the business still required to be administered and marketed.

Eventually, the model failed. I became ill. Cancer treatment resulted in my having a severe stroke. I don't blame the business I blame myself.

No two business models need the same hours. Tradesmen may find themselves still working 8 - 5 and doing administration in the evenings.

No matter what your business model, you are going to work hard to succeed. You will work smart to survive in the longer term. At times you long for the 9 to 5 and times you can celebrate your new life. Owning and running your own business is a different lifestyle. Be prepared for that. Different phases at different times may create many lifestyles. I remember a successful businessman, forced to sell his lovely new family home to raise vital cash. Only a year or two later he bought an even nicer home.

Pitfall 40 Butterflying

Entrepreneurs by definitions are ideas people. That in itself may be the biggest challenge. A friend of mine works for such an individual. My friend is the 'doer' in the business. The business owner no sooner launches a scheme when another one springs into his mind. The business is diverted on to the new scheme before the value is extracted from the previous scheme.

In the long term this does not work until the business is wealthy enough to resource these different threads. As a small business owner, this is wasteful and destructive.

Each idea takes time, effort, resources including money. Those around you whether family, friends, partners or employees who don't share this butterfly approach will grow tired and exasperated by this. Those employees who share this feature, you don't want in your business.

Generate a list of your ideas and pick the one that will be pursued to the exclusion of all others until its conclusion.

Keep a list of other ideas to come back to when the first is finished. View you job, as keeping everyone on the plan until the plan has delivered its maximum value.

There will be times when ideas are needed within the business to overcome challenges so save your innovative thinking for these.

If the business grows rapidly employ a manager to run with the idea and mine its value. To ever grow a saleable successful business this is an essential piece of advice.

You can move on to other plans while your manager grows the core business. This takes skilful recruitment to employ the best person in place. If the business can run on employed staff the business is able to be sold. If an enterprise can only run with you present the business is not saleable or at least not as valuable.

Appointing a manager to run your business profitably is the true test of the money machine. Make money as you lie on the beach or work launching a new business.

Pitfall 41 Reinventing the Wheel

When your skills and passion lie in doing a particular thing, we get distracted doing that at every opportunity, even when sometimes neither profitable nor necessary. This can be particularly prevalent for businesses that are grown out of hobbies. I can confess as a consultant, I spent too much time coming up with new and insightful products. I designed business processes, training course, all manner of smart clever approaches to problems that no one faced in reality. The time was better spent of speaking to potential new clients.

I coached an extremely capable web designer who too suffered from this problem. They spent a lot of time on their own website. Because they could code, they coded tools for every task. They recoded their accounting system and marketing process. Their third-party finance software was perfectly adequate and certainly did not need to be recoded.

When I worked for a major UK company, we needed a contracts data base to keep track of our hundreds of contracts.

The first one built by an external consultant was expensive, time consuming and never met our needs. The second one we attempted to replace the first even more detailed and of course more expensive but also never worked. This was as much our fault as the supplier. Each iteration had taken up hours of staff time. We explained what we needed and how we did our various tasks. This had to be interpreted into the consultant's model and coded into a database.

One day, a junior member of staff asked me for authorization of £250 to let him try something to sort the data base. This was approved. He came back 24 hours later with a data base that met the requirement 100%, it is still used today.

This was achieved this by purchasing an off-the-shelf database product which allowed some customization. This product developed by a major software designer, is the result of millions of dollars of development and real expertise. This prove to be a valuable lesson for us. The company received exactly what we needed by seeing the right approach and not reinventing the wheel.

My favourite story about this type of superfluous activity is about a colleague who met the CEO of a world leading American IT business who told this story to describe such work.

At Thanksgiving, every employee was given a turkey by the company. One year a young employee came to the boss and said, 'I calculate we could save considerable amounts if we bought a small farm and bred our own turkeys.'

The boss angrily replied; 'Never suggest anything like this again. We are an IT, business that is our focus, not running 'Turkey Farms'.

Henceforth, in the company the phrase ' Turkey Farm' described, out of core activity work that distracts from achieving strategic Objectives irrespective of whether profitable or not. Do not become involved in Turkey farms unless you are a poultry farmer.

Pitfall 42 A Reluctance to Decline Work

The most difficult step for a new business to take is to decline work. Time and emotion is invested in winning work the most difficult aspects for any new business; declining work is almost impossible to imagine.

Why would you decline work?

The work is beyond your abilities or resources.

You don't have the time.

You can't fund the cash flow.

The work may be a demanding, or for a difficult or untrustworthy customer.

The type of work lies outside your strategic aims.

The level of risk is not something you are prepared to take on.

Saying 'No' often prevents future big problems. If something feels wrong, it is usually wrong.

Key skills to be learnt including resourcing, funding or scheduling work. If you are able to identify the work to decline you will avoid angst, upset and reputation damage. Say 'No', apologize and explain why you can't take work on or bid for the work and help them to source a more suitable supplier.

Your objective is to protect your reputation and your business. Clients will respect your decision and offer you work in future.

As you became more experienced, include a decision point on any novel exciting work opportunity. Two questions: Does something feel wrong about this job? Should I walk away?

Pitfall 43 Poor Scheduling of Work

When scheduling work, you might want to say "Sorry, No, not now" and propose a future time when you can accommodate the work. This is better than having to explain delays or your non-appearance.

Scheduling issues often arise when there is no flexibility in your schedule. You want to fill your diary and maximize productivity and utilize resources. Delays, however caused, do untold harm to your business reputation. Include in your scheduling diary spells to catch up with late work or delays. They are a cost of doing business.

Some small businesses create a system of do parts of jobs and leaving completion for a later date. They rush off to start other work, running jobs in parallel. They imagine customers are kept happy by seeing their work started.

This is an inefficient way to operate. It is costly and in the end customers are unhappy.

Plan the job, the parts and equipment you need and turn up able to do the entire job to the end. Coming back to work takes time and effort is unproductive.

The same applies to taking on extra bits of work. For example, a painter is often asked could you just touch up something 'while you are here'. Anything that means more time, equipment, supplies or cost should be separately estimated and scheduled. If the task is indeed a quick piece of work that can be accommodated you can boost customer relations.

A key part of scheduling is to price additional work, called variations or change orders. If sizeable enough, do a new quotation. Minor extras can be handled by simply stating how much extra you propose which the client can accept or refuse.

Undoubtedly getting extra work from existing clients will be a source of additional income. Do not neglect to handle such extras in the form of scheduling and pricing. Many tradesmen are happy to do these for no extra cost knowing they are making a fair margin on the existing cost. If your price is fair and accepted a good customer have no problems with additional cost and rescheduling of variations.

Pitfall 44 A Failure to Comprehensively Cost

The most fundamental of business processes is costing. Accurate costing is essential to win work, utilize your resources efficiently, be profitable and succeed.

Your price must cover the costs associated with producing and delivering your product or service, plus that item's contribution to recovering the overheads of your business. It must not be too high which would result in insufficient demand and your resources being underutilized.

Costing is the point at which 3 of your key business processes meet. Marketing/Sales, Operations and Finance.

1. The Sales element is your bid /proposal to win the work.
2. The Operations Element is this is the point where you actually plan the work. That plan estimates the time and resources included in your proposal to win the work. To achieve this plan the steps of the work must be listed and hence this will ultimately be the foundation of your work scheduling.
3. The Finance element calculates your costs to put in the bid, tender or price.

Whether your business provides services or products or a combination of both, the same applies.

Let's look at the example of installing a kitchen.

The costs directly associated with the job include:

The time and expenses associated with visiting to measure and estimate the work.

Time spent installing the kitchen.

Any materials used in the kitchen that you contract to provide.

In addition, the job must pay its share of company overheads including:

Vehicle costs

The cost of your offices and workshop

The depreciation of tools and equipment

Its share of office staff payroll costs

Its share of office overheads like telephones, internet, stationery

Business rates, insurance, professional adviser costs

The job must also contribute to profit the reward for your investment in your business and money to reinvest in your business to improve its future success.

Some of these costs are fixed costs which means they do not vary with how many jobs you do. This includes your vehicle costs, which must be recovered across all the work that you do.

Other costs are variable dependent on the type of the job. Kitchen units are variable if you supply them the number of units changes the costs.

Your tradesmen time is fixed unless you employ them on zero hours contracts.

How you recover this depends on how you charge. The norm is to calculate an hourly rate for trades. Other types of business vary from hourly to daily.

A job that will take 100 hours your cost would be 100 times your hourly rate. Of course, your employees will incur travel time, time spent training, time with no payable work, time when you are paying sick pay when they will not be earning. You can see that this means that you need to cost at more than the payroll cost divided by the number of hours.

Let's take the simple example of a self-employed painter who has a limited company.

He wants to earn a salary equivalent of £40,000 a year.

His payroll cost will be:

- Salary £40,000
- Employers National Insurance Contribution currently at 13.8%. £5520
- Pension at say 4%. £1600

Total Wage Costs £47120

He will work 5 days a week for an estimated 44 weeks a year allowing for holidays, site visits to estimate work, non-productive time. This gives him 200 chargeable days a year.

> NOTE: 200 chargeable days a year is tough to achieve. Working 5 days a week, 200 days is 77% utilization of time (Maximum available time is 52 weeks x 5 days). If demand is very high this might be possible.
>
> Your work needs selling, time to look at the job and prepare estimates and so on. Different client timings rarely fit together easily. In this example a lower figure might be wise, but we will stick with 200 for now. In other types of business 100-150 days might be a better estimate.

His Business overheads are £20,000 to include vehicle costs, office costs (working from home), depreciation etc. this will mean adding £100 to every chargeable day.

£20,000(his overheads)/200(chargeable days) = £100 a day

You might choose to include in the hourly rate the contribution to overheads. This means estimating how many hours you will work over the year and how much your total overhead is. The example below shows how this is calculated.

Our painter wants his business to make a profit of 15% to allow more to expand and to employ others in future and give him some leeway.

His *daily cost* is calculated as follows.

    Salary - £47120/200 days £235.60 a day

    Overheads - £22,000/200 a day gives £100 a day

<u>Daily Costs £335.60</u> (Salary plus contribution to Overhead)

Here is an example of how this might be used to create an estimate for a small simple job.

    Paint, filler etc is £200

    An allowance for brushes, depreciation etc. Is £50

<u>Material costs are £250</u>

He estimates the job will take 3 days to complete

I will add a 20% contingency.

His estimate is:

> 3(days) x £335.60 (daily rate including contribution to overheads) = £1006.80 + materials £250 = £1231.80
>
> Contingency is £246.36

Total cost is £1478.16 + profit margin of 15% is £221.72

<u>Lump Sum Estimate is £1699.88</u>

Before submitting, the painter might ask himself. How risky is this estimate? Is there enough safety margin between my contingency and my profit margin?

Secondly, he asks. Have I too much contingency or should I reduce my price to be more competitive? In both cases the confidence he has about the time estimate and material cost estimate that will determine how comfortable he is about any changes to costing.

Scoping

The first stage of any work is calculating how much time a job will take. List every single task and put a resource against each. Some tasks may be done by time served tradesmen, others by apprentices and trainees. Now ensure that you allow for travel, lunch breaks and the like. Do your men sometimes go to wholesalers to pick up parts and consumables. Do some jobs need them to come back to your workshop? Do you need to include some contingency for uncertainty about the job or due to delays caused by other trades on the same job?

How accurate you are may depend on whether you are charging your customer an hourly or day rate or charging a Lump Sum. On bigger jobs for other businesses a more comprehensive contract might allow you to charge for variations if site conditions or other trades cause delays.

Pricing is a key skill; you can learn but if you do not possess or develop this skill you endanger your business.

Depreciation

Items you purchase and own need replacing over time and this replacement cost is called depreciation. Taxation rules govern how much you can allocate to depreciation each year but irrespective of that include depreciation in your costings.

Workshop machinery and owned vehicles and office equipment depreciate. A charge is made for this depreciation somewhere in your costs. The van will eventually need to be replaced and the money must be accumulated to pay for that.

These items and other aspects of your work also need to be charged for, small tools, consumables, maintenance and repairs. These hidden costs need allowing for somewhere in your costing. Petrol to access the job, without care you can easily forget these hidden costs. If you do not account for small expenses you will overpay tax, they will accumulate and detract from your profits. Profitable work will become loss making over time.

For Sales. Following a successful piece of work delivered. Will the customer give you more work? If none exists might they recommend you to their friends?

In Operations, you review the work to ensure the work is specified in your schedule and to see if anything can be learnt and applied to future work. For example, did tidying up take longer than you had estimated? Did you underestimate this or is there something special about this job? What might you do differently in future estimates?

In Finance, you prepare and submit your final invoice. Review the estimate at this stage to ensure that you made the profit you anticipated and if you did not understand why.

Costing and the associated processes lie at the core of a successful business. Some of your estimates will be detailed and accurate, others you will be confident to be less detailed.

I would always recommend doing a detailed estimate, too many tradesmen fall into the trap of making a quick response when asked:

"How much to do abc? " A snap response of £x at that stage will tend to be wrong in either direction. Better to say I will give you a detailed figure tomorrow/next week/later"

Pitfall 45 A Failure to Charge Enough

When I first set up my own company, I calculated the income I needed and based my day rate on that. I wanted £1250 a day. My employer who I was leaving offered me a 3-year contract of 48 days a year at £850. I happily accepted this because it guaranteed me a steady income at a fair rate for multiple day's work as I got my business off the ground.

A friend who consulted for Motorola said that she could secure me as many days as I wanted at £250 a day. I said told her my day rate. She laughed and said in Scotland £250 is the 'going rate'. I held out for £1250.

Except for long continuous pieces of work. I never went below £1000 after that initial contract.

My rate went to £2000 and even higher as I provided expert high-quality services. My clients saw business value in what I provided. No one ever felt they received poor value and my clients gave me repeat business. When we looked to employ other consultants, I discovered the £250 a day group consisted of retired bank managers, civil servants and junior accountants.

I needed the rate I charged to cover the unpaid days. In my case as a consultant 100 paid client facing days is about what could be managed in a year. The other days are for marketing, preparation and follow up of client facing days, travel and research.

My working assumption with new businesses I coach is that they are undercharging. Why, because I find this is invariably the case.

First: They fail to take account of all their costs in building their price model. I mention elsewhere the absence of contingencies. Costs increase as lessons are learnt. (such as the kitchen fitter who realized his first act in any job is to bin the enclosed cabinet fixture and use quality screws, hinges etc. in their place to deliver a quality product). New costs are identified (additional insurances and the like).

Second: New businesses are reluctant to charge what often seems to be a lot compared to their previous employee salary which they are more familiar with.

Economics tell us that lower prices bring higher demand. These are sales that new businesspeople desperately seek. Unfortunately, high sales do not equate to high profits if the pricing is poor. You are seeking the right balance. This is difficult in markets awash with new entrants who reduce prices to win work. In doing this they damage the market for other well priced businesses. Other businesses faced with cut price competition need to find novel solutions to highlight the quality of their product and the value delivered.

Under-pricing in itself can be counterproductive.

Illustrated by the story of a UK based washing powder company SURF who suddenly slashed their price, to position themselves well below any other product. Now one washing powder is much like any other, however rather than boosting sales, sales slumped dramatically as consumers thought that at such cheap prices Surf must be a poor-quality product.

Recovery is difficult once branded as poor quality.

Pitfall 46 Poor Commercial Process

A common cause of failure is the failure to understand and implement commercial process. This is understandable as Contracts are not an area of expertise that many people outside of perhaps lawyers and quantity surveyors possess.

These skills cover:

Taking instructions for work or in business-to-business situations receiving tender documents.

The next step is estimating or making a proposal or bid covers the following areas:

The Work

The Prices

The Terms and Conditions

The Work

The scope of work is covered in a tender or proposal if you have made a detailed one. For private clients, you will do any necessary measurements and site examination. Then produce a detailed work programme. List what is included and itemize clearly anything that is not included. Are you or your customer providing components? This must also be specified.

In this section that you specify how long the work should take. Access required and anything else that impacts how long a job will take.

The Price

Having established the work scope and priced the job, you provide prices in either the form requested or your usual method.

There are several ways to cost work.

Lump Sum

The preferred option now is Lump Sum pricing. Lump Sum is a single price for the whole Scope of Work to be delivered. Customers like the certainty but for you there are many occasions where a Lump Sum is not appropriate. You might not know how long the job will take until you get started. This is often the case where site conditions are difficult to account for. An example might be doing work on a wall or floor where until the current plaster or flooring is removed you don't know the condition of what is behind it.

Hourly or Piece Work

I employed a roofer recently. He charged a per square metre rate for installing a new flat roof which included both labour and materials. The scaffold was a Lump Sum charge.

My painter charges an hourly rate plus materials at cost. Hourly rates cover you well where you might not be able to estimate how long work might take, due to access issues or interfacing with other tradesmen on the same job. Clients are nervous about these because they do not know how much a job will cost until it is finished.

Use hourly rates with contractors you know well and have used before.

Cost Plus

Cost plus is when you provide the client with your hourly labour costs and source material you provide receipts for purchasing. You also give a percentage that you will charge on top of the cost price. Customers can be nervous but ought not to be. It guarantees your margins. This is not a common approach.

Variations

Should a customer ask for additional work you should charge for this where it goes beyond the agreed scope of work. This is not an issue where you are charging hourly rates or cost plus. On a lump sum job, you need to specify rates for variations. This might be an hourly rate provided in your proposal which include your profit margin. Material and parts would be specified at cost plus something.

What happens if you arrive to do work and can't get access because another contractor is working in the area?

These pricing approaches each provide advantages and disadvantages. Often you might end up with a combination of different pricing mechanisms. Experience and client preferences will affect this.

Estimates are just that. An estimate of what the job will cost but once made customers will expect you to only charge the amount estimated. The best practice should a job start going beyond the estimate is to communicate with the customer. Communication is the single most important factor in keeping clients onside and happy.

Having run through Pricing, it should be apparent that fully describing the work is fundamental.

On a recent job a contractors' work scope was confused and unclear. In the end I detailed the scope by email in response to his proposals. In the form of; 'You are going to do x, y and z. Your price includes a, and c but excludes this and that. It is amateurish and does not give confidence that the contractor is reliable or would do a professional job.

Commercial performance is as important as the quality of your work in establishing reputation.

Payment

On a longer job or a high-priced job, it would not be unreasonable to get a deposit before starting and to get milestone payments as key stages get completed. Milestone payments will help you to keep cash flow positive and will highlight to you if customers are having financial difficulties. In the worst case will reveal occasions where you should not put any more time or money into a job.

Terms and Conditions

The last part of your proposal are the terms and conditions that would form the contract with the scope and prices.

There are many types of terms and conditions depending on the type of work. Your industry body might provide standard contract terms, or a lawyer might draft these for you.

Include if a price includes or excludes taxes such as VAT in the UK or sales Tax in the US.

I would always include payment terms. e.g., 15 days from completion. Advance payments or a milestone schedule of payments.

If you provide materials, such as kitchen units for example, your terms might mention that you retain ownership until paid.

The most complex area in any contracts is liabilities and insurance. If you possess insurance highlighting this to the customer can add to the benefits you are offering and give you the edge over other suppliers. I do not employ tradesmen in my house who do not have insurance. Nor should anyone.

I do recommend that you have a contract with your client. A lawyer will draw a standard one up before starting your business and always use it. You imagine that you will never need to use it, but you are mistaken. There are times you might choose not to enforce it with good clients and in some circumstances. There are other times you will be glad to use it.

A business I advise is run by two young computer programmers. On three occasions clients did not pay or insisted they had not delivered the work, demanding a refund. Twice these clients decided to bully them into paying despite knowing that they themselves to be wrong, and they raised small claims in court. The business had well drafted contract and went to court, resisted the charge which was dismissed and were awarded costs.

Pitfall 47 Failure to Use Professional Advice

Many businessmen and women are reluctant to use professional adviser because of the perceived cost. There is a time and place for professional advice. Professional advice is money well spent if you intend growing a sizeable successful business.

A lawyer can advise you on the legal structure and can set the

company up, registering names and protecting any intellectual property you own like designs, inventions and trademarks. They can give you draft contract forms to use in your commercial dealings either contracts or purchase orders.

Accountants in the case of a limited company must audit and sign off your annual company accounts. They will prepare these from invoices, bank statements and receipts that you keep. They can advise you on costings, loans and how to manage your tax for the employees, yourself and your company. Many also can provide company set up services.

Your accountant can prepare your annual Company House returns and be your registered office. They might act as your finance director on an ad hoc basis. They can keep your accounts on a weekly basis and provide management information. Accountants now offer to provide book-keeping services for reasonable fees. Accountants can advise you on bookkeeping software and set it up for you, if you chose to keep your own accounts. They will tend to recommend the software they are familiar with and if you are using an accountant this saves time and cost.

If you can use their services and as a result dedicate more of your time to income generating work this is money well spent.

Modern accountancy software works well but software does not give you advice. Purchasing software depends on the type of business you are running and how comfortable you are yourself in bookkeeping. Is your time best spent doing your business or doing the accounting? My wife kept my business accounts on a daily basis for my smaller businesses, and she did the *Pay As You Ea*rn (PAYE) and Value Added Tax (VAT) returns. Both services an accountant might offer to you.

Create and develop your relationship with your bank. Banks now do not accommodate this preferring an online model. If your turnover is high and you borrow money it is likely you will be given a personal manager. My philosophy is for there never to be surprises for the bank manager. If things change from what a forecast, tell the bank manager before they discovered it.

Professional advisers can be a sounding board. They help many similar and dissimilar clients. They advise companies you want to emulate and have seen issues that you need to avoid visits to advisers are a useful focus point to assemble any information to present and update them. They see things in a business that you might miss or not be aware of.

Your business. professional advisers may also act as your personal financial advisers which works well.

You might also consider personal financial advisers. The Financial advisers looked after pensions, investments and personal insurance. Some useful and others not.

Pitfall 48 Beware the Cerberus

The importance of being able to pat your head and rub your tummy simultaneously.

Most new businessmen and women lack business training.

Doing the work is well understood but the other key aspects of running a business are much less familiar and often ignored, omitted or minimized to the detriment of the business.

A failure to meet legal requirements and deadlines can end up with huge amounts of time and money being required to put things right.

Administration can be easily ignored with so many other things to do. Put the right systems in place from the outset and it can run efficiently and effectively. This allows you to focus on your business performance and to sleep easy at night.

The Cerberus was the 3-headed monster of Greek mythology. It guarded Hades. It is synonymous for a beast composed of disparate parts. There is an important parallel in business especially new and developing business. The different nature of the parts requires particular care.

The 3 heads in business are the Executive the Operative and the Corporate.

Executive: Plans and sets Strategy and monitors and redirects the business.

Corporate: Keeps records, keeps accounts and submits annual reports and the annual accounts. It chases debts and administers the business. It does the business record keeping the hundreds of daily repetitive tasks.

Operative: Is seen as 'Doing the business.' An artist produces art, a photographer takes pictures a shop keeper serves customers.

Too many businesses focus too much or even exclusively on the Operative. Whether it be selling your product or producing your product or delivering your service it is most often the area you feel passion for. This is the element you enjoy doing and often to the exclusion of all else. This head is your favourite monster, and you look after it well.

The converse of this is that the business owner started the business to escape the tedium of the boring administrative stuff a part of any job. It is human nature to avoid doing the things you don't like doing.

The trouble with 3 headed monsters is that if you focus on one head, the other two are flailing around behind you and can bite you when and where you least expect it.

The Corporate head bites hard, sometimes very hard. A failure to submit annual statutory accounts for a limited company can result in a criminal prosecution, a fine which increase every day you are late and can be as much as £5000. A failure to submit VAT returns or the annual company return also raise fines and sanctions.

These sanctions are only part of the problem, if you don't keep accurate current records you don't know how the business is performing are you making profits or losses? Money slides out unnoticed and unrecoverable and many young businesses head to liquidation or their owners to bankruptcy for a lack of attention. Keep current and set time aside to do it.

Alternatively, budget to employ advisers who are skilled, disciplined and even passionate about these things. An accountant is important and gives you someone to be answerable to in submitting your records for them to complete and keep updated.

This process can pay for itself if you get your expenses, mileage and sometimes losses offset against tax. Discipline is worth money, its absence costs money.

The Executive head of the Cerberus is also important. It sets the plan and the strategy and monitors progress against it. The business plan is the blueprint for your business, supported by the budget. It is your map to success. If you don't know where you are going it is likely you won't get there. You must know why you created your plan and if it is failing, what mistakes or wrong assumptions you made. Only then can you change these and set a new course. For these reasons your plan and budget must be kept current.

Create a Business Plan, and a Budget before you start. Measure how you are doing against this plan, and more specifically your Objectives. We entrepreneurs are over optimistic, our progress may be slow compared to our projections but is our plan working? Are we solvent? Realistically will we continue to be solvent on the path we have chosen.

To do this measure actual income and expenditure against the metrics and budget we created to back up the plan. Only by entering the actual numbers do we move from our imagined projections to reality. This is welcome. We now are working with real data against which to test our business and to make any corrections, we need to ensure our success or protect from disaster.

The projections and budget need revisiting monthly or at worst quarterly. Don't make this a time-consuming exercise just enter the accurate numbers and review their impact. The key issue is the differences between your forecasts and your actuals the so-called variances. Does this change your outlook?

It may be that you cut some expenses or do more marketing, but it is vital to measure and revisit these variances, early before they become irreversible.

A major revisit is needed annually. To reset your Objectives and Budget and to create new plans and direction.

There are hidden dangers also in the Operative head. Is your product or service taking too much time to create? Is it costing more to make than you are selling it for?

The joy of creating our cherished product or service, our desire to be recognized for producing excellent work can obscure the fact, that it is uneconomic in its current form. Free work, samples and display pieces are not work and certainly not sales.

The more the business becomes focussed on the Operative head, be wary of it becoming a hobby or vanity business, an excuse to buy more equipment or materials. The figures tell the story of which monster is prevailing or not.

Pitfall 49 Ignoring Legalities

When you are busy with work and excited at the prospect of new clients, chasing after legal formalities can often be left to wait. The trouble is that governments and local authorities do not wait. They employ staff and have the systems to chase you up. Once you get into a cycle of missing key deliverables the time and cost of sorting this becomes substantial.

In the UK Companies House require annual company returns for limited companies. The tax authorities require your accounts to be submitted on time and payments of Corporation Tax, PAYE and VAT to be made on time. Industry bodies which licence you to

operate need your membership kept active. Different industry regulators need health and safety returns etc. to be submitted on time. There are dozens of items which require to be administered including payments to insurers and others to keep your business running. Even smaller things like vehicle licences, insurance and MOT need to be processed. Bills require to be paid.

Too many new businesses fail to appreciate the hassle and distraction a failure to keep updated can bring. Your business can be closed or suspended, or you could face legal action. The more serious consequences of failure can be catastrophic or terminal to a new business or even an established one.

A diary is a low-cost investment but pays dividends if properly used.

Employ your accountant to deal with Companies House and the Tax, Customs and Excise Departments. Accountants are disciplined and organized for keeping on top of these areas.

Should you forget or just be unable to provide the information on time - admit this at the earliest opportunity, as a priority. Official bodies will be understanding, if advised in advance of any issues and can even be helpful if kept informed.

I cannot emphasize more any issues should be met head on however embarrassing before they escalate. This is one of the best rules to abide by.

Pitfall 50 A Failure to Manage Risk

If rule1 is 'don't lose money', rule 2 must be 'don't lose large amounts of money'.

Let me tell you 3 horror stories.

I employed a small local builder to build me a deck. They were wonderful workers, well priced an excellent find.

I needed some more work done but could not contact them.

A friend told me they had gone out of business. They had taken on a big kitchen job locally and had burned down part of their customer's house in the process. I don't know if they went bankrupt because they did not buy insurance or if they lost tools and equipment they could not afford to replace. Perhaps this big job provided the only income for that period and the loss of those revenues destroyed their business.

I was of course disappointed for them and hope that this salutary tale helps someone avoid this.

The second story is about a small IT Business. It had considerable expertise, growing slowly despite late payments amongst its clients and other teething problems. They won a big contract with an overseas government. This seemed to be the breakthrough they needed to grow. To complete the work, they took on a couple of subcontractors. The early signs seemed to be healthy, and payments came in steadily. Suddenly as the contract ended the payments slowed down. £30,000 remained outstanding which was never paid.

The business continued close to insolvency, struggling through always chasing cash.

Eventually they closed, all their debts paid, but the struggle proved too much, and the business closed to redesign its approach.

I hate these horror stories.

There are two things to do, when launching a new business. Firstly, even at the Business Pan stage prepare a Risk Matrix as previously described.

Brainstorm all the risks, assessing the probability for each and the likely adverse impact it makes on the business. List actions to mitigate that risk. There are always actions to take. If you identify and act on these in advance, there will be no regrets.

Pitfall 51 A Failure to Insure

I will say a little about insurance as this is so important for a Business. Do not take this as definitive advice, I do not know your detailed circumstances. engage a reliable insurance broker. I include this section to prompt you as to the type of insurances to consider. Different sectors need different cover, and I could not cover these comprehensively. Your industry body is a starting point for advice and sometimes offer insurance cover tailored to the industry members.

How you insure depends on two initial things.

First, The legal structure of your business. Is the business a legal entity in which case there is some protection of your own assets? Is the business just you as a sole trader? If so, your home, bank balance and future may be at risk.

Second, Your contractual arrangements. If you work against agreed terms and conditions your liability and that of your customers ought to be specified. A contract ensures that you know that you need insured and what you are protected from.

It is often reported that a fire will bankrupt a business. An uninsured claim in the early stages will bankrupt most.

It hits your profits and reputation. You need additional money to replace stock, tools, equipment. In the case of fire or flood you lose trading time and income if you close down.

Uncomfortable as it is, contemplate these catastrophes. It is not the time to adopt the ostrich position!

Company Insurance

If you are a limited company, limited means limited liability. Your liabilities are limited to the value of assets of the company. Its property, equipment, stock and money in the bank plus money owed to you. You can only be made to pay that far, beyond which the company goes into liquidation. You lose your business and its assets but that is it. Subject to some rules of which debts rank most highly including tax, secured loans and salaries in some cases.

Types of Insurance

EL/PL

You will hear brokers talk of EL/PL insurance. Simply this stands for *Employers Liability and Public Liability*. This is obtained as a combined policy.

Employers Liability

Employers Liability covers claims by employees for injury, illness or death caused in the course of their employment and in the UK is compulsory.

Public Liability

Public Liability covers claims by individuals injured or killed by you or your staff or who are injured or killed as a result of visiting your premises or by employee's actions in their property. If a customer falls downstairs, tripping over a loose piece of your carpet, your public liability insurance meets any claim.

Public Liability is bundled with Employers Liability and it is a fair price for cover up to £2-5 Million.

Professional Indemnity

Businesses who provide professional services which advice clients rely on require to carry *Professional Indemnity* which covers losses resulting from poor advice or incompetent service. This applies to lawyers, doctors, financial advisers, architects, consultants, engineers and so on. In some cases, professional bodies provide and administer these insurances. Professional Indemnity (PI) is expensive insurance, but the need and amount depend on the exposure.

Product Liability

If you provide or manufacture goods or products or include these in your service this is an important insurance. Imagine a butcher who poisons customers with E.coli or a toy manufacturer whose product causes harm to a child. This liability can address short and long-term effects from any product. The cost depends on the type of product that you supply.

Pharmaceuticals are a high-cost insurance, golf club suppliers less so.

Fire, Flood Theft and Loss of Profits

If you own your own premises, workshops or warehouse and valuable stock, a property fire, theft and flooding policy would be prudent. If you rent, be aware of your landlord insurance arrangements for this and how this effects your business. Many rental agreements put some insurance obligation onto the tenant.

This is often packaged with insurance covering loss of profit, because of the disastrous impact this has on a business.

Key Man

If your business depends on you or other key individuals there is a category of insurance called key man insurance. This provides financial cover for when a key man is ill or unable to work. How readily they can be replaced in the short term is key to whether you insure or not.

Insurance for Employees

Larger employers tend to offer a personal insurance package for their employees. A typical package might include:

Death in Service typically three- or four-times salary.

Permanent Health which provides ongoing income beyond what a company might provide in sick pay, for long term illness or disability. Permanent Health is an important insurance to hold if you are self-employed.

Other Insurances

The normal insurances also apply. Your property and vehicles need insurance. You can insure against employee theft of money and many other less obvious things some of which your individual business might demand others of which just add to your costs.

It can seem a maze but a realistic consideration of exposure and discussion with a broker can put together an affordable package for the stage your business is at.

Insurance for legal costs has become more important. Businesses and individuals hard-pressed for cash turn to litigation where they feel that they are poorly served by suppliers. Defending such actions whether genuine or frivolous takes time and money and is best left to professional. Legal insurance is often packaged with other insurances or services.

Insurance needs constant review as you grow.

Some insurances are legal requirement, some are contractual and others to give you peace of mind. Others you hold as a responsible employer.

There are a number of employers who avoid having insurance to reduce costs. This is a false economy. Insurance makes you a more attractive contractor and a more attractive employer.

Pitfall 52 A Failure to Manage Profits

One poorly understood part of running a developing business is a failure to manage profits.

A recommended services model is 1/3rd 1/3rd 1/3rd. This related to fees charged to clients. The First 1/3rd covers salary, the second the business overheads. The final third is the reward for taking the risk of being in business and return on investment.

Many young businesses fail to set their prices high enough to deliver this final third. Fearing overpricing might lose them work they operate 1/2 a 1/2 model. The first half pays the costs of the business and doing the work. The second half pays salary. This model inevitably fails with the first business set back such as a large non-paid bill, an urgent need for a repair or a replacement of equipment. Setbacks are inevitable and only reserves can help you to survive these.

In the absence of reserves, you end up borrowing money. in these circumstances which you don't have the extra returns to repay the loan and interest or you start chasing clients to pay early and damaging your reputation. Robbing Peter to pay Paul is fine until Peter needs paying. This tactic generates a downward spiral with each mitigating step making it worse and accelerating the downward trend with the inevitable outcome.

Without generating this extra return and reserves results ultimately in failure. The wise are patient, generating more business with what appears to be less competitive prices than your under-priced competitors. In time they will fail, and you will survive and pick up their lost clients at acceptable margins in the future.

Coming back to the final third in the model. It gets distributed in various ways. Some goes to reserves. The rest can get paid out to the owners as profits as dividends, a tax efficient way to take additional 'salary'. On both distributed profits and reserves in the UK tax has to be paid. The reserves sit on your books available to meet any issues or to distribute in future without further tax to pay.

There is an argument that if you are making money, keeping money in reserve is reducing your potential income. Whist a valid argument, the cautions about needing reserves as a protection against future problems still applies.

Pricing and estimating must account for these reserves or you are not running a sustainable business. It is this growing reserve fund that permits you to grab growth opportunities and so on. I remember winning my first seven figure contract. The elation was tempered when I looked at the cash flow on it and realized it would take £40,000 to fund the cash flow. The bank wanted security on my house to lend me the money. In the end I funded it from my own money and my business reserves.

Pitfall 53 A Failure to Recruit Well

There is a time and place for employees. To be able to provide employment to hard-working individuals is rewarding to them and to you. Employees can be both the source of pleasure and of frustration.

There is logic to having employees to allow you to be more productive, to leverage their time to increase your sales and profits and to provide expertise that you lack. You want employees that treat your business as you do but not all do. Small businesses attract employees who enjoy the excitement of new business but sometimes think that they could do it better.

In my largest business, at the outset, our ability to recruit consultants was awful. With only a few exceptions our recruiting turned out to be a disappointment. This had to be our fault not theirs. A few recruits were exceptional. If we learnt lessons it would be:

Young enthusiastic support staff who anxious to learn proved the most successful. We also brought in expertise that we ourselves did not possess.

We failed when:

We recruited in a hurry.

We failed to do proper due diligence.

People had run their own business before but failed.

Taking these in order.

Rushed recruitment doesn't work. We identified people who we instantly liked but ignored obvious issues. If a recruit mentioned a talent at sales and our eyes would light up but, in most instances, they never brought in a single job.

On other occasions we accommodated projects and spend on the individuals pet themes which sounded promising but later just turned out to squander time and money.

Poor due diligence was our worst failing. It is embarrassing to admit that we actually employed a facilitator who was deaf in one ear. If there is a faculty you need for facilitating it is sharp hearing. A simple pre-employment medical would spot this issue. We did do this after that problem and also employed a company that provided pre-employment checks against a variety of issues. Money well spent.

Those with experience of running their own business seem good employee prospects, but the question is why did they not succeed? It is often the same flaw that might leave you needing to dispense with their services at a later date.

Parting company with employees is a complex, expensive and frustrating process. We prided ourselves on being fair. At least twice individuals took advantage of us. In both cases we felt awful about the parting process.

Conversely, providing stimulating employment opportunities is one of the greatest pleasures in running your own business. It is wonderful watching employees grow and flourish. It is less rewarding when they suffer through your failures.

The only solution is to make the right decision at the outset. If possible, get a professional to screen applicants and do the initial interviews.

The model I now use is to only employ support staff, secretarial and accounts assistants. I use professional firms for professional services, accountants as finance directors. For operational staff positions I employ self-employed consultants. This has worked really well. It works well for all parties. The consultants are grateful for the work which often being unable to generate work for themselves. We share the rates I get for them equitably. I am transparent about the rates they are charged out at. All employment relationships must be WIN: WIN.

Section 6. Finance

Finance Essentials

A well-executed Forecast in the Business Plan

A Budget

Proper invoicing and credit control processes

Prompt accounting and record keeping practices

Prompt official returns for Business and Accounts

Systems for reviewing Cash Flow

Initially a business launches with its Business Plan. From that plan a Budget is developed listing the areas of expenditure anticipated and provisioned for. The Sales Plan then provides the Sales Forecast of income. Both of these are estimates and are reviewed and updated throughout the year to be aware of your cash flow and profitability.

The Budget provides the foundation to monitor income and expenditure and note variances against. The Variance is the difference between what was Forecast and the actual numbers. This allows the business to accumulate money required for forecast future expenses, technically called accruals.

You keep track of income and expenditure as the year progresses to have a current record. The record must be current so that at any time you know your exact financial position.

By bringing together income and expenditure an analysis can be generated against which to make decisions to change track to increase income and profit and decrease expenses or to invest in more resources or stock. This is called the Management Information System.

You cannot run a business well without accurate financial information. In all but the smallest and simplest of businesses, an accountant is a sound investment, and many provide economic rates for providing an ongoing service.

You, your Finance person or your Accountant prepares Management accounts to inform decision-making on a monthly or annual basis.

A Management Information System informs you of:

Monthly sales by category

Monthly expenditure

Cash Position

Profit or Loss

Position for year ahead of or behind forecast

Upcoming work

Upcoming expenditure

Late payments: 30, 60, 90+ days late

In this way a monthly meeting or an evening at your kitchen table, can decide on steps to address finance issues early.

Chase up late payments. This is simple administration, prudent and ensures cash flow and the effective use of money and time. Management tools include staff utilization and the sales pipeline. A balance between present and future is important at your review meetings.

Variance: Keep track of differences between your Budget and reality. Keep your Budget updated as real information arises to better predict the future of your Finances.

'You must keep score'

Imagine a cricket match where no one keeps a note of the score. At the end who knows who has won. The biggest pain for most Businesspeople is bookkeeping but cannot be avoided without storing up problems and costs. It is not helpful to find at the end of a match that you lost by 3 runs. Better to know how things are going during the match to make appropriate changes. The same applies in business.

My solution was to work hard enough and keep sufficient cash reserves, to know I was always ahead financially.

An essential element of your Finance system is to keep track of all expenditure including payroll and taxation. Monitor the payment of bills and record every expense and payment including cash. Monitor prepayments and accruals to ensure that cash flow is managed throughout the year. Your Finance system ensures that accurate and comprehensive records are kept along with supporting documentation such as invoices, receipts, mileage undertaken etc. Please keep your own money and that of your business completely separate. I always had a separate business credit card to keep track of expenditure and ensure I only used business money for business.

Pitfall 54 Parsimony

Every business requires money. I have worked with over-spenders and under spenders. Both issues are as bad as the other and undermine long term success. A failure to invest in proper equipment results in losses and the appearance of not being professional about your business. Frugal habits and caution are not the same as parsimony or not being prepared to make necessary expenditures. Tools are an example. Professionals use professional quality tools.

Investment (spending on items that your business can generate profits from), can feel a dangerous and a risky business step. What does the situation really require, and will that investment bring returns? What is lost by not investing? For the non-businessperson investing can feel like gambling. This is why working out the possible upside compared with the risks is important. Don't gamble with your business. A well-thought-out plan identifies where money may be invested to secure an acceptable return. Investments must bring in profits. Throwing money after a problem rarely solves it and often makes matters worse. Work out the best outcomes and the worst outcomes before investing and in both cases what you would do next. Would the bank lend you the money based on your business case?

A business case or a cost-benefit analysis is a study that demonstrates benefits over cost. Do a cost-benefit for a single investment decision: an office, a vehicle, a new employee, a piece of equipment, software any investment with an impact on your profitability. This is a sort of mini business plan.

For the cost of investing, what benefit is achieved? Can you demonstrate that your numbers are favourable in every circumstance? A cost-benefit analysis for any big investment pays dividends. Remember that if you had to borrow the money you would have had to pay interest. Businessmen and businesswomen need investment to make profit on top of the interest the investment ought to return.

The old is expression says - 'to make money do so with other peoples' money'. Where else might you get the money? Nowadays there are a variety of online lenders, from business lenders to using crowdfunding. No prudent businessperson would ever use payday loans or any other high interest loan.

Write the cost-benefit and take it to your bank to see their response. They might even give you some ideas on how to fund things. What reason might the bank refuse the loan? Are you better funding it yourself or borrowing from family and giving them interest?

Be a professional investor in your own business. Consider if you would make more by investing elsewhere.

Never be scared to invest and always invest prudently must be your motto.

In the early stages of a business only spend what you need to spend. Don't buy unnecessary stuff, buy quality but not flash? Manage your overheads wisely.

It is always easier to spend money than to make money. Purchases are easier to make than sales. It is always so easy to justify why you must buy something. Human beings are expert at justifying why they must have something. I am a black belt in this racket! Starting a business is no different. I know. I can build a plausible case for buying equipment or software despite knowing I could muddle through to the time when the business can afford it and fully justify its purchase.

Remember every penny of your business income you don't spend goes straight to profit, either increasing profits or decreasing *losses*. Be competent at this and you will sleep better at night. It is easy to think that money spent is offset against tax. This is severely flawed thinking, you are not in business to offset tax, you are in business to make profit.

Every penny spent has a tendency to create other costs; insurance, maintenance, depreciation, storage requirements, and replacement costs. A bit like the mother of a friend, who bought a larger freezer which eventually resulted in their building an extension to their house to 'accommodate it'. I cannot deny that I have fallen into this trap, we all do at some time.

Ideas for justifying spending against potential future earnings is a major trap. " A complete video suite might allow us to sell videos of our training courses" it might, but you might never do that, and it might distract you from running training courses profitably!

Pitfall 55 Over Stocking

Too much stock is a flaw in many new businesses. Retailers reluctant to miss any sale, fill their shelves with every conceivable product. Tradesmen fill they workshops and vans with every tool, manual and power tool that they ever want or need. Food businesses fill their fridges and larders with enough food to meet every conceivable possibility or the most optimistic demand level. Their menus offer dishes for every potential client, the range is too large and poor order numbers results in food stocks deteriorating or becoming less fresh. Restaurants stock ingredients for dozens of items on their menu where a smaller number might make more business sense.

Overstocking, ties up working capital leaving the business short of cash to meet its other costs. Worse still the products and consumables stocked become obsolete, out-of-date or even deteriorate and become unsaleable. Hardware is replaced by better models and so on. 90% of the capacity or capability of some items is never needed e.g., over specified computers.

Customers given unlimited choice, find it more difficult to decide, and can fail to buy.

Unnecessary stock takes up shelf space and can become difficult to trace when needed.

Obsolete stock needs to be sold at a loss and if not takes up valuable shelf or storage space.

To understand stock look at the fruit and vegetable sellers or the flower sellers in a market. They must buy and sell all their products in as little as 24-48 hours. Products not sold deteriorate and become unsaleable. How rapidly must you turn your stock to convert cash spent back to cash in the bank?

Overstocking has a parallel in staffing - over staffing. No business can afford to employ staff who do not earn money and profits for the business. You would not employ staff who sit on the corner doing nothing, yet some businesses happily buy stock that sits on a shelf gathering dust.

Choose your niche. Monitor where demand really lies by recording what is bought and when. Stock turnover rate is a vital performance measure. Equipment also must earn its keep. The restaurant that bought an exotic piece of equipment or the joiner who bought an expensive routing table must both review how often they are used. Not often? - then perhaps it is best sold to generate cash and free up some space, hiring equipment when required.

In many respects decluttering your business allows you to focus on what is important. Items for sale have elements of seasonality. Don't hold your winter stock beyond winter and certainly not to the next winter. Stock must be converted to sales not collected or hoarded.

Nothing can replace experience and record keeping in the area of stock.

I learnt about stock management from my father. He had a paint, glass and wallpaper business. It was a substantial regional wholesale outlet, and he had access to an unlimited number of stock items in paint and wallpaper.

He chose to specialize in 2 brands of paint (although there were many others available) with selected items from a couple of specialist smaller brands. He chose these brands as being appropriate for the quality market: one directed at professionals the other at a domestic market. My father stocked the entire range from the big two brands and constantly rotated the stock. He bought more before his trips to the largest buyers and in the spring and summer months when demand was at its peak. No more than two or three pots of any size were left on the shelf when new deliveries arrived. Those colours that did not move were not replaced. Sometimes he was short of stock, but the order was marked incomplete and the item quickly requisitioned, and the order fulfilled.

Wallpaper had a much larger number of options. He stocked 100 papers. 50 patterned and 50 plain to match. He selected these from the 5 big suppliers and made up his own wallpaper book which he gave to all his trade customers. In his showroom he held twenty additional wallpaper books, papers which he could readily source but did not stock.

This approach allowed him to bulk buy paint and wallpaper to achieve the best prices. He was able to turn the stock into immediate sales while learning what sold and what did not. Monitoring changing trends and maintaining the best-selling lines all the time.

The same applied to staff. His painters worked above 90% of the time and when they had idle time, they freshened up the office or on rare occasions painted our own house. My mother complained that she waited years for our house to be painted the true measure of his staff productivity.

Pitfall 56 Failure to Manage Costs

When I worked in the oil industry in Aberdeen, it was said:

'How do you start a contracting business in the oil Industry?'

'Rent a smart office, buy 5 BMWs and then decide what business you are in and take someone to lunch and see if they will give you work.'

On leaving Grangemouth refinery to start my own company my boss gave me advice the day I left.

'Geoff, you will always be welcome here, but don't turn up in a nicer car than I drive.' His point was well-made. Clients are not impressed by flashy cars or offices. It forces them to think. 'I am paying for that; am I being overcharged?'

Conserve your cash and minimise your expenditure until you have built up a contingency fund for when business is tight, or problems arise. That way you sleep at night and have the chance to grow through problems and setbacks.

By managing cost, you maximize profits. Every penny not spent goes straight to the profit of the business or reduces the losses.

Some businesses are particularly wasteful on IT, the latest model of computer, high quality colour printers and lots of expensive software.

You can source economic computers that work perfectly well and even access free software. Items like this seem to be necessities for a business but more than anything cost management will see you through difficult times. Challenge yourself on minimizing your costs. Can you run your business from home? What equipment might you share? What could you source second hand? What can you not spend?

Buy sensibly those items which must be bought. For a tradesman good quality tools are important as these are in daily use.

I once joined up my business with another owned by a friend. His turnover was four times that of my business, but he spent ten times what I spent on overheads. My business was much more profitable and more secure when times were hard. The joint business was a better fit with the joint overhead and allowed us to increase our turnover. There were worrying times when business was tight, but we got through. I would have run a much leaner organisation, made more profit and been less stressed. It was tempting to have better offices, powerful computers and more staff but a sound financial foundation still tops every other concern.

Pitfall 57 Bad Cash Flow

Cash Flow is the rate that money comes through your business, coming in and going out. Positive cash flow, your goal, means at any given time you have a sufficient cash balance to meet expenses as they arise and are due to be paid. Ideally this occurs without having to chase around for money, charging early or doing cheap work to generate instant cash.

Cash flow has a major complication beyond what I state above. You could be in profit with more money coming in than going out and still fail. Money must be received in time to meet expenses. You have a huge unforeseen expense in June, you cannot pay it with money you expect to earn in November. The business will not reach November as it would be insolvent in July.

It doesn't matter how profitable your business is if you do not have the money when you need it. It is tragic, how many profitable businesses fail because they do to have the money on hand to support the costs and outgoings which arise.

I have often looked at business plans where income over the period exceeds the expenditure. Periods arise when you do not have cash to meet the expenses because of how and when costs arise.

Rent, wages and buying materials keeps requiring funding through the year. If the nature of your business is that money comes in seasonally cash flow out your best seasons may be insufficient to meet your needs in slower times.

The parallel is the home budget. Salaries come in regularly, but expenses are either steady like food or occasional such as insurance, Christmas, summer holidays or unexpected car repairs. Unless money is laid aside for these big expenses they cannot be paid on time. The same applies to your business. A good budget and forecast with some built in contingency funds ensure that the cash is available when required. If you pay out £3000 for insurance every December, you have to accrue £250 every month to ensure that in December the money is available to pay. Accruing is the act of putting money aside to meet future expenses.

In a business, employee wages, rent and rates must be paid on time or you will face court recovery procedures.

If you supply or use parts in your business, your suppliers may extend short term credit although many will not until you establish a track record. Take the example of a kitchen fitter. They might require kitchen units, electrical and plumbing items. Unless the client will pay a deposit, they will need cash to purchase these items before they are paid for. You will need to cover wages or payments to employees or subcontractors. This must be planned for and cash allocated for these purchases without which you may not keep your business running.

If you sell, three kitchens to fit in the same period? Can you fund this?

What if your client pays a couple of weeks late? Can you fund the time?

Cash is King

You will hear businessmen and women use this expression. Cash Flow is possibly the single most important finance issue for the new business. Cash flow problems can be created by poor credit control, in other words customers not paying you for the goods and services you provided them.

Cash flow is the difference between your income and expenditure on a daily basis. You see this in your Bank Account. The issue of waiting for payments to clear must be monitored. Understand how long payments and receipts take to clear your bank so that you know at any time your cash position.

You might be lucky and own a cash business. You know if you have money or not. A market stall is a cash business, things are paid for immediately with cash.

Payment delay has many aspects to it. If a customer goes into liquidation or administration, you might never be paid or receive a very low percentage. Worse still you might run out of money before receiving what you are owed as your own costs don't stop.

A factor called precedence arises here. Should a company go bankrupt there is a ranking order amongst debtors.

The order of getting paid is first the insolvency practitioner who handles the process, then secured creditors such as banks, others with security documents, unsecured creditors, tax man, suppliers, customers and lastly shareholders. This may vary from country to country. Your business may come well down the list along with the other unsecured creditors including HMRC (the tax man) Worse it may take months for you to be paid and it may only be pennies in the pound.

It is vital to keep on top of cash flow and late payments and act on time.

The second issue for cash flow and one of the most common cause of business failure is over trading. You might think rapid growth was what you would want. This is not always the case. Fast increasing orders might mean you need to employ more staff and buy more of the product input goods and services. If you are paying out for these things before you are paid for your sales, you can see how without cash reserves you would soon run out of money. The more quickly you grow the faster you run out of money.

When you calculate how much cash you need to start your business it is important also to allow enough money to cover your costs as business builds up. You also ought to accumulate cash reserves, but this is often impractical.

Your budget must track the monthly cash flow which is your starting cash plus monthly income minus monthly outgoings. Track this figure through every month remembering to forecast seasonal differences. How will you cover any shortfalls? At times, I tracked my cash flow daily to know that I would always meet my outgoings.

In different industries and with different company sizes different payment practices exist. Large companies contract to pay on 30 days or more. That can be 60-90 days depending on if you submit your invoice promptly and your contact approves and processes it. Some companies delay for longer payment periods even 90 days and beyond, try to avoid these companies in your early days unless you have substantial cash reserves.

Build relationships with both your customer contact to expedite processing and the accounts payable person so that you understand and can push for your invoice to be on the payment run. The two key contacts are firstly, the person who approves the payment and secondly, the Accounts Payable individual who processes your payment. I once employed an accounts assistant, Clare was great at contacting and befriending these people. She kept on top of our cash flow and it improved dramatically. Clare could tell me where a payment was in a client system, which payment run it was on and what date it would reach our bank. This was invaluable.

This is a lot of work, which can be stressful and is a skill you will perfect but may not like doing. It takes great administration skills and good interpersonal skills to be good at.

You may be able to employ a person to deal with this full time as your business grows. They are among the lowest paid employees but are worth it, if they are good at it.

The ultimate protection is to hold cash reserves.

You can 'factor' your invoices, but this costs money from your profits. In factoring, you submit your invoice to a factor, you bank may offer this service. The factor pays you immediately, when you submit your invoice to a customer, deducting their fee from the payment recovered from your customer. Your payment record, industry sector and company size will decide the fee charged which can be high and of course reduce your profit margin. You can also employ debt collectors of differing types. Lawyers and courts are your last step but are expensive and if there is no money to collect you will often waste money in trying.

Factoring has one major pitfall in that the factor has their own debt recovery process. It will be rapid and often quite aggressive. Your late-paying customers might not appreciate this approach and you may lose them.

You also need to understand accruals and prepayments. If you make annual payments your business must be accumulating the cash to make them on time. If you collect money on the government's behalf in employee taxes like PAYE or VAT. It is not your money and not strictly part of your cash flow, except insofar as you must pay out to the government when it is due.

Keep your tax in a separate bank account which you never touch except to pay the government. Keep VAT, employee salary taxes and an estimate of corporation tax if you are liable for this. The money will be there ready to make the payment when it is time

to pay the tax man. No stress ever.

Pitfall 58 Bad Debt Control

Credit control and the consequences for cash flow is of paramount importance to any business. It must be the prime responsibility of one person. Promptness of action is paramount it cannot be allowed to slip. I divide my thoughts into 5 areas.

Before Contracting

Before entering into a contract, a policy must be established to ensure the other party can afford to meet their payment obligations Appropriate checks ought to be made. For individuals and small businesses, a credit check ought to be made. An assessment can be made of what the impact would be if the company fails and what assets exist to recover against. The larger the contract the greater the risk to your business, the more need for pre-contract checks. It is remarkable how few businesses do credit checks. They lose focus in the excitement of winning new work and cross their fingers hoping for the best. Many credit agencies will give advice on a customer's solvency and provide insurance against things going wrong and money not being paid.

A UK government scheme exists for overseas work called the Overseas Credit Guarantee Scheme, which is worth researching for overseas work.

A deposit for work with stage payments allows work to be undertaken with positive cash flow and work halted if payments are missed.

When Contracting

No work should be commenced without a signed contract. The contract needs to be specific about being able to charge interest on late payments otherwise you cannot do this.

During Work

Set the prompt payment process in place. Ensure invoices are sent out to arrive on or before the date payment is due to meet the payment rules.

Larger companies will have a complex procedure with invoices being passed into the next month for payment if they don't arrive for example by the 15th day of the month. Understanding this process is important.

Credit Control

A Credit Controller becomes a key position in any company doing more than say £200k p.a. turnover. At some point it must become a dedicated position. Generally, it is an individual with a college accounting qualification who reports to the Finance Director. In most cases you are the credit controller!

They need a policy to operate:

Who chases late payments?

How aggressively?

When ought your credit controller refer the debt to a Director/Owner/You?

When to send out reminders and Final Demands?

At what value or time to commence debt recovery processes, who to use. At what point legal and court proceedings are initiated?

The timeliness of these processes needs constantly monitored. A reputation for prompt financial recovery is no impediment to sales except to those customers you do not want.

Chasing Overdue Invoices

A collection mechanism ought to be put in place. Giving financial limits, time limits and steps to be taken on overdue payments.

Options are:

Internal Action

Debt Collection Agencies

Direct Court actions with diligence after judgement

Lawyer actioned which often takes only a letter.

Understanding the nature of your customer base is key. There are 'can't pay' and 'won't pay' clients. There is little point pursuing 'can't pay' unless they own assets to send Sheriff Officers after. 'Won't pay' must be encouraged to pay. 'Can't pay' needs you to secure such funds there are before another creditor gets at them.

You can adopt a carrot and stick approach prompt or early payment gets a discount. Late payment means interest and action.

Stopping work before incurring further expense is incurred is a prudent step. To stop the work must be a specific right under your contract. A customer breaching a contract is not justification for you breaching it as well.

Your best payment collection methodology is a good personal relationship backed by a consistent structured collection process.

Pitfall 59 A Lack of Capital

Some business ideas need money to succeed. If you are paying high costs to rent property or equipment and the interest rates are very high, perhaps the model it is better to borrow the money to buy these items. You might try subletting or sharing their use with others. Capital is rarely cheap but by owning things outright may give you the flexibility you require for a successful business model.

A common failing is to get Capital for a business and then spend it badly. Capital must earn its keep like any employee or piece of equipment. Capital must earn more than it costs in interest. If it requires repayment that money must be gradually laid aside to accumulate for when it is repaid. Remembering that loan payments are a fixed cost, they need provisioning for before lean times so that payment can continue to be made.

The other thing you might desperately need is working capital. If you are in a business where the model is profitable, but it takes a long time for your income to come in, you will need working capital. This is money to pay those bills requiring payment in the short term before the income associated with them comes in. The interest rates to be paid on working capital must be factored in your pricing of course.

Examples of businesses needing working capital, include manufacturers who must buy raw materials or components long before the finished items are paid for. Businesses whose clients demand credit for 30 – 90 days also need working capital. Some seasonal businesses need working capital to get them through the slower periods.

Another consideration for the new business is the matter of security. To receive capital funding the lender may well want security over the assets of the business or commonly for new businesses over any personal assets of the business owner. This is a risk that must be managed. Losing your business is bad but losing your house may be much worse.

Often lenders will ask for shares in a business if its prospects look good. It is tempting to give shares to get capital, but the consequences must be thought out. In larger businesses the lender might also insist on representatives on the Board of Directors.

In a growing business giving away shares may be surrendering a lot for a little but if the capital is vital it might be the essential step to take. Input from the lender with their contacts and expertise might also prove invaluable to a growing business as in Dragons Den. Giving future profit, value and control away might be a trade off against succeeding in that growth. Consider the outcome in both good and bad scenarios to judge the value of getting capital. Your accountant can give you advice on this decision and its consequences or alternatives.

It may be a more difficult decision if your business cannot grow without the injection of capital. The question is 'Will the business grow faster with the capital?

The difficult question is ' Can we just make do without capital by moving more slowly? Be wary, there are times to invest owning less but growing faster and more securely and there are times to walk away. The faster more secure route is tempting and indeed lenders base their offers on this. Like all business it is a trade-off and a negotiation.

Your goal is to accumulate sufficient reserves to be able to provide your own capital. With every investment required you should still decide whether to invest your own capital or to borrow from the ban. This allows you to keep your capital for future opportunities or to give you security for future difficult times.

Pitfall 60 Lack of Sustainability

The pandemic has highlighted a major flaw in many businesses. A failure to maintain a sustainable business model, to provide a safety net for difficult periods. A difficult period can include unexpected expenses and unpaid invoices. Problems often come in groups. Be prepared for several occurring simultaneously. There are several components to this. We cannot foresee every disaster but there are some common features.
Cash reserves are important. If your business had to shut down and could not earn, how many months of overheads can you afford from your cash reserves?
If you had to stop working from your premises have you an alternative channel for sales such as online trading?
If you are taken ill and cannot work are you insured or do you have a fully competent replacement? What insurance protection for lost trading do you have?
How quickly are you able to dramatically reduce your overhead costs?
Your risk matrix will anticipate some big problems, but nothing beats financial prudence and an escape strategy particularly alternative means of generating money in your business.
The businesses I advise know that I stress the value of reserves.

My Offer to You

If you find my approach to be helpful, my commitment to you is to do everything in my power to help you to become extraordinarily successful.

We can offer a number of ways to help.

We can review your business plan and give you input and advice of ways to maximize profits from your idea and spot associated opportunities.

We can give you an annual mentoring package, providing video calls on a monthly basis, tailored to your exact requirements.

We offer a coaching package based on 12 monthly modules with video calls and downloads covering the four main business areas highlighted in this book of Planning, Sales and Marketing, Finance, Operations and Administration.

A package includes a download to be completed and discussed with a Mentor in a video or telephone mentoring call.

Email me at geoff.anderson@derson.co.uk to arrange an appointment to discuss a package or to receive more information.

You can interact with us on our Facebook page Passionate Profit. We will be delighted to hear from you and to answer your questions there.

www.ingramcontent.com/pod-product-compliance
Lightning Source LLC
Chambersburg PA
CBHW070622220526
45466CB00001B/76